Mary and Archie Tisdall have had a life of travel which many would envy. Archie served in the Royal Air Force for 40 years and during this time they lived in such diverse countries as Singapore, Jordan, Libya, Tunisia and Malta.

Towards retirement they bought a motor caravan to enable them to visit further places abroad, principally in western Europe, and gradually they began to write of their experiences for magazines.

They have travelled extensively in Spain, spending many winters in the Canary Islands. This resulted in 1984, in the publication of two guide books: *Tenerife and the Western Canary Islands* and *Gran Canaria and the Eastern Canary Islands*.

Their love of Spain has taken them many times to the Balearic Islands. The outcome is this book and a further two guide books: *Majorca* and *Menorca*.

They have two sons and two daughters, and when not travelling they live in Salisbury, Wiltshire.

Shy Ibicenco maid, be no longer afraid.
The yellow ribbon you wear in your hair
Is it for a brave corsair?
They drove the pirates out to sea,
Ibiza now is happy and free.

(Authors)

Acknowledgements

The authors would like to thank the following people and organisations for their help, directly or indirectly, in the preparation of this book:
The Spanish National Tourist Office, London; Señor Antonio Munar Cardell, Director General of Tourism, Majorca; Señor Juan M. Sanchez Ferreiro, Press and Public Relations, Tourist Board, Ibiza; Thomson Holidays Ltd (Lesley Rawlings) Ibiza; Hotel Directors, including Compañia Hotelera del Mediterraneo (CHM hotels) Ibiza and Sol Hotels Ibiza; Brittany Ferries, Plymouth; and the Trasmediterranea Shipping Co, Madrid.

Our thanks go to Yvonne Messenger, our helpful editor, and to our publisher, Roger Lascelles. Finally we acknowledge the interest and encouragement from friends and family, with a special mention for our son Nigel, who controlled our affairs so well.

Maps by Joyplan Cartographers, Chessington, Surrey.

Front Cover: Puerto San Miguel, on the north coast of Ibiza, provides a quiet anchorage for yachts.

Ibiza
and Formentera
A Traveller's Guide

Mary and Archie Tisdall

Roger Lascelles, Cartographic and Travel Publisher
47 York Road, Brentford, Middlesex TW8 0QP   Telephone: 01-847 0935

Publication Data

Title	Ibiza and Formentera, A Traveller's Guide
Typeface	Phototypeset in Compugraphic Times
Photographs	By the Authors
Printing	Kelso Graphics, Kelso, Scotland.
ISBN	0 903909 67 7
Edition	This first June 1988.
Publisher	Roger Lascelles
	47 York Road, Brentford, Middlesex, TW8 0QP.
Copyright	Mary and Archie Tisdall

All rights reserved. Other than brief extracts for purposes of review no part of this publication may be produced in any form without the written consent of the publisher and copyright owners.

Distribution

Africa:	South Africa —	Faradawn, Box 17161, Hillbrow 2038
Americas:	Canada —	International Travel Maps & Books, P.O. Box 2290, Vancouver BC V6B 3W5.
	U.S.A. —	Boerum Hill Books, P.O. Box 286, Times Plaza Station, Brooklyn, NY 11217, (718-624-4000).
Asia:	Hong Kong —	The Book Society, G.P.O. Box 7804, Hong Kong 5-241901
	India —	English Book Store, 17-L Connaught Circus/P.O. Box 328, New Delhi 110 001
	Singapore —	Graham Brash Pte Ltd., 36-C Prinsep St.
Australasia:	Australia —	Rex Publications, 413 Pacific Highway, Artarmon NSW 2064. 428 3566
	New Zealand —	David Bateman Ltd. P.O. Box 65602, Mairangi Bay, Auckland 10 (9-444-4680)
Europe:	Belgium —	Brussels - Peuples et Continents
	Germany —	Available through major booksellers with good foreign travel sections
	GB/Ireland —	Available through all booksellers with good foreign travel sections.
	Italy —	Libreria dell'Automobile, Milano
	Netherlands —	Nilsson & Lamm BV, Weesp
	Denmark —	Copenhagen - Arnold Busck, G.E.C. Gad, Boghallen, G.E.C. Gad
	Finland —	Helsinki — Akateeminen Kirjakauppa
	Norway —	Oslo - Arne Gimnes/J.G. Tanum
	Sweden —	Stockholm/Esselte, Akademi Bokhandel, Fritzes, Hedengrens. Gothenburg/Gumperts, Esselte Lund/Gleerupska
	Switzerland —	Basel/Bider: Berne/Atlas; Geneve/Artou; Lausanne/Artou: Zurich/Travel Bookshop

Contents

Foreword 9

1 Introducing Ibiza and Formentera
Islands of contrast 10 — Situation 12 — Climate 13 — When to go 14 — What to pack 16 — Budgeting for your holiday 17 — Tourist information 17 — Some places of special interest 18 — beaches 20

2 Getting there
By air 23 — By sea 25 — By rail and ferry 30 — By coach and ferry 30 — Yacht club facilities 31

3 Where to stay
The star rating 32 — A selection of hotels and guesthouses 33 — Apartments and villas 39 — Package holidays 39 — Camping and motor-caravanning 40 — Taking children to Ibiza and Formentera 41 — Travel agent services 44 — Property purchase 45

4 Getting about the islands
Roads 47 — Rules and recommendations for drivers 47 — Servicing and repairs 48 — Road signs 49 — Petrol stations 50 — Self drive car hire 50 — Scooters, mopeds and bicycles 51 — Taxis 52 — Bus services 52 — Ferry boats 54 — Coach excursions 54

5 A to Z information for visitors
British consul 56 — Churches 56 — Communications 56 — Currency and banks 58 — Electricity 59 — Fire precautions 59 — Hairdressing 59 — Health 59 — Laundry 60 — Medical services 60 — Newspapers and magazines 62 — Police 62 — Problems and complaints 63 — Public conveniences 63 — Radio 63 — Shopping 65 — Souvenirs 66 — Television 69 — Time 69 — Tipping 69

6 Food and drink
Food 70 — Drinks 74 — Bars and cafés 75 — Restaurants — 75

7 Leisure activities
Sports and pastimes 80 — Museums and art galleries 84 — Nightlife 85

8 The Islands
A short history 87 — Ibiza and Formentera today 91 — The Ibizan way of life 94 — Music and dancing 96 — Fiestas and folklore 98 — Island flora 99 — Wildlife 102

9 Ibiza town
Dalt Vila 104 — Sa Pena and La Marina 109 — Ibiza, the modern town 111

10 Touring Ibiza: the south and west
Playa D'en Bossa and Las Salinas 117 — In and around San José 119 — Cala Vedella, Cala Bassa and other beaches 122 — San Antonio 123

11 Touring Ibiza: the north
Ibiza town to Portinatx 125 — In and around San Miguel 128 — San Mateo and Santa Innes 131

12 Touring Ibiza: the east
Jesus and Cala Llonga 135 — Santa Eulalia del Rio 136 — Es Cana and Punta Arabi 138 — San Carlos 140 — Cala San Vicente and San Juan 141

13 Formentera
Ibiza town to Puerto La Sabina 143 — San Francisco Javier 145 — Cala Sahona and Cabo Berberia 146 — San Fernando, Es Pujols and the Caves of Xeroni 147 — Playa Mitjorn and Playa Es Arenal 149 — Es Calo to Faro de La Mola 150 — Las Salinas and nearby beaches 150 — Cana Costa and La Sabina 152

Finale 154

Appendices

A	Spanish-English vocubulary	155
B	Windforce: The Beaufort Scale	158
C	Useful conversion tables	160
D	Bibliography	164

Index

The lifelike statue of Isidoro Macabich Y Llobet the Ibicenco historian, sits with his open book on a bench at the side of the road in Dalt Vila, the old city of Ibiza.

Foreword

Ibiza, the third largest island of the Balearic group, is also known as Eivissa. Included in this Guide Book is the little known island of Formentera, which lies five kilometres south of Ibiza. A number of place names have variations of spelling, where necessary Spanish and English versions are quoted, generally they correspond with the Firestone Map T26 or E54, from which road numbers, distances and heights are taken. The currency exchange rate at the time of going to press is 220 pesetas to £1, which should be taken into account when assessing costs.

The purpose of this guide is to enable the visitor to know where exactly Ibiza and Formentera are situated, how to get there, and when to go. Places of interest for all types of holidaymaker are described in detail, including buildings of historic merit as well as the fine sandy beaches and quiet coves.

Much is written here to help the tourist have a pleasant stay. The various types of accommodation are explained, local prices are quoted, shopping areas, markets, souvenirs and good buys are suggested. The costs of car rental, taxis and coach excursions are given. The many sports and entertainment available in the resorts are listed.

This book describes interesting day drives that allow visitors to enjoy places away from the beaches. Both Ibiza and Formentera are islands where walking is enjoyable, so routes are suggested.

The Ibicencos are justifiably proud of these beautiful islands with their historic culture, natural beauty, fresh clean air and warm climate. They are happy to share such an abundance with all who return year after year, to see again Ibiza and Formentera and, of course, to have a good time.

ONE

Introducing Ibiza and Formentera

These two islands in the Mediterranean seem to have dual personalities, because of the way they combine old customs and a country way of life with a modern outlook that welcomes the individual spirits of today. Though they are free and easy, a sense of balance prevails, so that holidaymakers from all walks of life find here most of what they desire.

Islands of contrast

Easily reached by air and with frequent passenger and vehicle ferries, both these islands are blessed with a very favourable climate. The hot summer sunshine overhead is often tempered by sea breezes along the sea shores. Magnificent beaches, washed by translucent calm waters, make bathing and sea sports enjoyable for all. Lush fertile valleys of orange groves and pine forests lead along quiet roads to medieval churches and villages. An abundance of bars and restaurants offer a splendid variety of drinks and cuisine, with local specialities tempting the palate and purse.

For the young at heart, Ibiza town and San Antonio provide a cosmopolitan way of life, with a casino, live shows, cabaret, music bars and discothèques. There are plenty of bright boutiques, *artesanias* (craft shops), souvenirs and sports centres, so there is never a dull moment. Even the warm nights throb with life.

For those seeking a more restful time, Formentera offers the atmosphere of a desert island, with long beaches of white sand and empty roads. Here you become very much aware of sea and sky, and experience a sense of being very close to nature. No one hurries here; days drift by as sand trickles through your fingers. Even the salty water that comes from the taps reminds you that you are on a small island, short of the precious fresh liquid.

Formentera's sustaining fig bread (*pan de higo*) with its almonds is the perfect snack for tourists to take on their walks along the beaches. And Formentera's thick wool provided by its sturdy sheep and sold not in balls but weighed in the old fashioned hanks is excellent for knitting a chunky sweater to be worn in the cool English climate.

Whilst in Ibiza you will have the opportunity to do lots of things that are different. You can go on a Donkey Safari, over the mountains on a surefooted creature that will cause you at first to laugh in despair trying to get it to move at all; but laughter turns to shrieks when the donkey realises that it is homeward bound and breaks into a fast trot, you bobbing up and down in the saddle — no stirrups for this ride. Typically Spanish *sangría* will bring a rosy glow to your cheeks, especially if you try and drink it from a *porrón,* a traditional glass or pottery container with a long tapering spout. You must tilt back your head and let the liquid flow into your mouth, not letting the spout touch your lips — not as easy as it sounds. You can experience a ride on a camel (very different from a donkey ride!) or at least have your photograph taken beside one of these creatures of the desert. Maybe you will try your arm at archery, rifle shooting or French *boules.* Do not be surprised if you find yourself in fancy dress, playing at being Tarzan to some strange Jane, all is good fun.

Whether your holiday resort is a large cheerful hotel complex or a quiet guesthouse in the mountains, where the wild herbs and heathers grow by your bedroom window, you are sure to find that the more often you visit, and the longer you stay, the greater will be the joy of knowing the pineclad white islands (*pitiusas islas blancas*) that are Ibiza and Formentera.

Visitors to Ibiza and Formentera, January to August 1985	
British	258,936
German	194,942
Other nationalities	240,023
Total	693,901

Situation

Ibiza is the third largest of the Balearic Islands, which lie in the Mediterranean, near the outlet to the Gulf of Valencia. It has the distinction of having the only river in the Balearics, Santa Eulalia del Rio. It is 41km long and 20km wide, a total area of 572sq km, slightly smaller than the Isle of Man. A mountainous island, the highest point is Atalaya (475m) while its 99km of coastline comprises high cliffs in the north and long stretches of pine fringed sandy beaches with sheltered coves elsewhere.

Formentera, five kilometres south of Ibiza, is the fourth largest island of the Balearics with an area of 100 sq km. It is roughly one fifth of the size of Ibiza and is really two islets joined by a sandy isthmus. At the widest point, Formentera is only fourteen kilometres from east to west. Its highest point, La Mola, is just 192m.

Both islands belong to Spain and the people (about 70,000) speak the same language. The islands are, however, very different: Ibiza is hilly and verdant with much cultivation in the valleys, while Formentera has dry open land with expanses unsuitable for crops, where only a few fig trees and a small amount of wheat and vines are grown.

Ibiza can be reached by sea and air. Modern ferries make the crossing from Barcelona (280km) and Valencia (170km), and also from other Spanish ports including Palma, Majorca (140km). Regular and charter flights link Ibiza with national and European cities (London is 1805km). There is no airport on Formentera but it has a frequent ferry service with Ibiza, the crossing taking about one hour.

Geographically Ibiza and Formentera are nearer to the coast of North Africa than to Barcelona: the water-wheels, windmills and flat-topped white houses scattered throughout the islands are reminiscent of Moorish villages. Being centrally situated in the western Mediterranean the islands have been used by many people in the past. This remains so even today.

Both Ibiza and Formentera have several small inshore islets. The three important ones close to Ibiza are **Isla de Tagomago** which lies off the north east coast between Es Cana and Cala de San Vincente. There is no sandy beach but there is good swimming from wooden jetties. Off the west coast and opposite Cala Bassa, is **Isla Conejera**; legend has it that the Carthagian warrior Hannibal was born there. Although it is possible for boats to land, swimming off the island can be hazardous because of sea urchins, whose spiky quills can inflict a painful wound. **Isla Vedra** stands out dramatically 282 metres from the extreme southwest tip of Ibiza. Uninhabited, it is the haunt of sea birds, goats and wild flowers.

Formentera has three islets of note. First, there is the small **Isla de Ahorcados** (Hang Island) where, in the past, criminals and pirates were hanged and left as a fearful warning for all to see. One passes close to this islet on the ferry crossing between Ibiza and Formentera. Second, a little to the east is the larger but deserted **Isla Espardel**. The third islet is the beautiful **Isla Espalmador** where yachts moor and beach parties visit; its white sands make it a picture postcard desert island. At low tide it is possible to walk between Espalmador and Formentera, but local guides warn that the swiftness of the incoming tide makes this dangerous.

Climate

The climate of both Ibiza and Formentera is mild for most of the year; only for a short time in winter is the average temperature lower than in mainland Spain. They enjoy about 300 days of sunshine each year, with more than ten hours a day in summer. But the nights, even in summer, can be cool and a light jacket may be required. In winter there is about five hours' sunshine a day. Humidity is stable at about 70 per cent throughout the year. Temperatures seldom fall below 40°F/5°C or rise above 90°F/32°C. The almond trees in blossom in early February are an unforgettable sight.

Most of the winter's rainfall comes in sudden showers that fill the cisterns and clay subsoil. Until recently there has been no shortage of water but with the increase of tourism sometimes during the month of August the tap water can become decidedly salty. This is especially so in Formentera where there are no hills to collect the moisture or to protect the land from the cold Tramontana winds, and the shortage of water becomes quite a problem and a deciding factor against further developments.

The splendid Mediterranean light and brilliant summer sunshine bathe the islands with a luminosity that, coupled with the white-walled houses, can be quite dazzling. But a walk in the sweet pinewoods or a rest under the swaying palm trees will soon refresh you.

When to go

Although Ibiza and Formentera have a mild climate compared with north European countries, during the winter months from November to March the majority of hotels, apartments and guest houses are closed. At the beginning of April the whole scene changes when the package tour operators commence their flights. During April and May the climate is spring-like and the winds on some days are quite fresh, so that it is better to find a sheltered position where the sun feels warm.

June onwards sees the clear blue skies and cloudless days. The midday sun is very hot and at times it is essential to protect the body from over exposure. This is especially so during August and care must be taken with young children and those with sensitive skin.

Climatic chart		Air temp average	Sea temp average	Days of sunshine
Jan	°C	12	13	26
	°F	54	56	
Feb	°C	12	14	14
	°F	53	57	
Mar	°C	13	14	21
	°F	56	57	
Apr	°C	15	16	15
	°F	59	61	
May	°C	17	16	28
	°F	63	67	
Jun	°C	22	21	28
	°F	71	71	
Jul	°C	25	24	27
	°F	77	76	
Aug	°C	26	26	31
	°F	79	80	
Sep	°C	22	22	28
	°F	72	73	
Oct	°C	20	20	19
	°F	68	68	
Nov	°C	16	18	24
	°F	61	65	
Dec	°C	13	16	28
	°F	56	61	

Based on information from the Spanish Tourist Office in Ibiza

Rain is rare during the summer but an unexpected storm can blow up, catching visitors unawares, so a light raincoat or umbrella is a useful thing to pack. Autumn sees the leaves turning and the fields of vines a glorious hue of reddish brown. By the end of October the tourist resorts are quiet and many shops are closed.

Should you wish to visit Ibiza during the winter months bear in mind that accommodation is limited. In Ibiza town the two four-star hotels, Los Molinos and Royal Plaza, are open all the year. There are three hotel apartments open — El Corsario, Estrella Del Mar and Pitiusa — but the only meal served is breakfast. On the rest of the island winter accommodation will be found in one- and two-star apartments. The campsites are closed from November to April.

Winter accommodation is available in Formentera, at Es Calo there are two hotel apartments, the Escandell and Pinormar, open all the year. The one-star *pension* Capri, in Es Pujol, is open but does not provide meals other than breakfast.

During the summer school holidays many hotels and flights are fully booked, so it is advisable to make your reservations well in advance for July and August.

San Antonio Bay provides lots of sunbathing, safe swimming and entertainments.

What to pack

Depending on the time of year of your visit to Ibiza or Formentera choice of clothes will vary from the lightest of summer wear to woollen garments. From June to September you can count on hot weather every day. But you may need a cardigan or wrap some evening or when it is windy. The most comfortable fabric for hot weather is cotton or other natural fibres; if you use the easy care manmade synthetics, then loose styles will feel better. The same applies to footwear: do not take tight fitting shoes, as feet will tend to swell in the warmth. However, for walking in the country strong shoes are required as the ground is very hard and stony.

Nowadays the wearing of bikinis, even topless, is becoming accepted on the quieter beaches. But when walking in the streets a shirt or cotton top should be worn over swim wear. Churches no longer require women visitors to cover their heads, but a decorous manner is expected.

Evening wear is mostly casual; in the four star hotels men may be expected to wear ties and jackets. When you go to an evening barbecue excursion some sort of shawl or jacket may be needed as you will probably be eating outside.

Remember to take a sunhat or glasses (though these can be bought locally). Suntan oils and creams are a necessity unless you are already very tanned. Some anti mosquito cream may be useful, too. No need to pack quantities of toothpaste, soap or shampoo as plenty of brands are sold on the island though prices can be higher in some resorts.

Even the most amateur of photographers will wish to pack their camera. There is a potential for marvellous holiday snaps. If you wish for something of better quality, remember that the strong light, the white houses and sparkling seas will require a light density filter. All popular sizes of films are available, but with prices generally higher than at home. In the resorts, a forty eight hour development service is usual.

English paperbacks, newspapers and magazines can be purchased, though usually at double the UK price. A Spanish/English phrase book will be useful if you wish to make contact with the Ibicencos, especially when visiting inland towns and villages. Travel will be enhanced if you take binoculars, there are many opportunities for distant viewing. In the northern and eastern parts, many wild birds can be observed in their natural habitat or migrating.

If you are a pipe smoker you may wish to bring your own favourite brand as some imported tobacco is hard to find, many foreigners feel that Spanish pipe tobacco is a bit on the rough side. Cigarette smokers will probably arrive with their duty free smokes bought on the aircraft. Most Spanish cigarettes are made of strong black tobacco. Nearly all popular brands are sold at twice the price of the domestic product. If you are self-catering and drink a lot of tea, you may wish to bring your own supply of tea bags, they are expensive in Ibiza and Formentera.

Budgeting for your holiday

The cost of living should not prove higher in the Balearics than in Europe or the UK. Generally speaking, package tour holiday-makers require spending money for entertainments, drinks, and possibly additional meals, unless the package include full board. You must allow for extra costs such as taking part in sports and excursions, the hire of sun umbrellas and chairs, laundry and tips (*propina*) for waiters, taxi drivers, maids and porters. Maybe you will need some extra film for the camera and for buying souvenirs and gifts.

Prices in tourist areas will probably be a few pesetas higher than elsewhere but if you take into consideration the extra cost of travelling to a non tourist place to do your shopping, it will probably work out much the same.

For the independent traveller it is possible to live quite cheaply by buying local foods. Chickens, eggs, cheese, fruit, tomatoes, cucumbers and many drinks are less expensive than in the UK. Bars and restaurants are less costly and generally give a cheerful and good service.

Tourist information

Visitors to Ibiza and Formentera require a valid passport which must be stamped with arrival date by the Spanish Immigration Authority on entry to the country. It is your responsibility to see that this is done, otherwise your entry is illegal. You do not need a visa for a stay up to ninety days, but after this it may be necessary. Information can be obtained from the **Spanish Consulate** (20 Draycott Place, London SW3. Tel: 01 581 5921). Up-to-date tourist information can be obtained from the **Spanish Tourist Office** (57/58 St James's Street, London SW1. Tel: 01 499 0901).

Vaccinations are not normally needed for Ibiza and Formentera. Only in the case of an epidemic would they be required. Visitors are allowed to bring in any amount of foreign currency or travellers cheques and up to 150,000 pesetas. You may take out of Spain 20,000 pesetas and foreign currency equivalent to 100,000 pesetas (£363).

There is a **Tourist Information Office** in the centre of **Ibiza** (Vara de Rey 13. Tel: 30 19 00). It is open from 0830 to 1300 hrs and 1700 to 2000 hrs, 0830 to 1200 hrs on Saturdays. Brochures and maps of islands and towns are given free. Written enquiries are welcomed. The Consell Insular de Ibiza y Formentera is at Avenida Ignacio Wallis. Tel: 30 43 04.

In **San Antonio** there is an **Oficina Municipal D'Información** at the eastern end of the Paseo Maritimo, in front of the Hotel Florida. The **Tourist Bureau** in **Santa Eulalia** is located in Calle Marino Riquer. It is open 0930 to 1330 and 1700 to 2000 hrs, Saturday 0930 to 1330 hrs. Tel: 33 07 28.

In **Formentera** the **Municipal Tourist Office** is in the Town Hall (San Francisco Javier. Tel: 32 00 32).

Some places of special interest

Ibiza

Approximate distances by road from Ibiza town are shown in brackets.

Cova Santa (9km) The Holy Cave, 30m deep and 210m long. On Ibiza to San José road; open to the public. The stalagmites and stalactites are all well illuminated.
Dalt Vila The old walled city of Ibiza, now a national monument and very well preserved. At every corner and alley way are interesting buildings. The view from the top of the castle walls makes the climb worthwhile. Visit the Cathedral, museum and restaurants.
Es Cubells (21km) Small quiet village on clifftop, south west corner of island. Fine sea views. Old church. Good but small bar and restaurants.
Ibiza Town A fascinating mixture of the old and new to be seen everywhere. Busy port and intriguing old fishermen's quarter, Sa Pena, now a hippy and tourist centre. Nearby casino.
Las Salinas (9km) Salt pans that are still in use and export 60,000 tons a year, helping the economy. See the salt being loaded on to ships.

Puif des Molins On hill top, close to city walls. Roman and Carthaginian necropolis. Nearby museum has art treasures and artefacts from the tombs.

Punta Arabi (24km) Situated close to Es Cana, on the road to San Carlos, Punta Arabi is a weekly Wednesday market, 1000 to 1700 hrs. Originally just a hippy market and visited for its colourful people, now a more traditional flea market.

San Antonio (15km) The most popular resort, it has a magnificent bay with hotels, shops, restaurants, boat trips and night spots. Definitely for the lovers of the bright life.

San José (15km) Important rural village with splendid eighteenth-century parish church. Souvenir shops include hand-made embroidery and lace.

San Juan (22km) A farming village near to the northern coast, on the road to Cala San Vicente. Pretty countryside.

San Miguel (19km) Delightfully busy village with large fourteenth-century church on hill top. Folkloric groups give exhibitions of singing and dancing in the square.

San Rafael (7km) Set in open countryside, this sprawling village has several pottery shops selling local ware.

Santa Eulalia del Rio (15km) The second largest town and still developing as an important tourist centre. On hill top, old white Church of Nuestra Señora de Jesús contains valuable artistic treasure. Museum. Good views of surrounding country and coastline.

Santa Innes (20km) Also known locally as Santa Agnes. This remote tiny northwestern village is at the end of a country road. Small church and two simple bar/restaurants.

Formentera

Approximate distances by road from La Sabina are shown in brackets.

La Sabina Only port. Used by ferries, fishing boats and yachts. Car rentals, bike hire, buses, taxis. Fishing from harbour walls.

Mirador Es Caló (12km) On one of the highest points of the island. From this place you can see across both east and west coastlines. Restaurant here sells fig bread.

San Francisco Javier (3km) Capital town. Main plaza has eighteenth-century fortress church, souvenir shops, supermarkets and restaurants. Quiet and friendly, a few street traders add colour.

Xeroni Cave (9km) Recently discovered and now open to visitors. Though small it has fine examples of stalagmites and stalactites, illuminated. Well worth visiting

Ses Salinas (4km) Sea water lake, yields 20,000 tons of salt each year. Road goes round salt pans and low pinewoods. Nearby Dolman, recently excavated, now protected by wall.

Playa Arenal (12km) Dirt track leads to *hostal,* then pine woods, sand dunes and beach bar.

Beaches

These are some of the best known beaches to be found in Ibiza and Formentera. The official nudist beach on Ibiza is in the south at Es Cavallet; another spot is unofficially used at S'Aigua Blanca, about four kilometres south of Cala San Vicente. Virtually all the beaches on Formentera are topless.

Ibiza

Cala Bassa Large, gently curving white sandy beach, with rocky inlets suitable for fishing at each end. beach bars. Reached by boat or bus from San Antonio.

Cala Conta Sandy beach with shallow water safe for children. Rocky terrain, no shade but beach umbrellas. Reached by boat or bus from San Antonio.

Cala D'Hort Peaceful, remote, small sandy cove with clear water. Reached by car down steep track from San José.

Cala Llonga Wide sandy bay with shallow water, ideal for young children. Sunbeds and restaurants. Reached by bus from Ibiza town and Santa Eulalia.

Cala Nova Sandy cove north of Es Cana, wild scenery. Sometimes the white-capped breakers can be dangerous with strong undercurrents. Good walking along tree shaded perimeter.

Cala Pada Good sandy beach, safe for children. Sunbeds, pedalos, sailing, windsurfing and beach bars. Reached by car or boat from Santa Eulalia.

Cala Portinatx Most northerly beach, the *cala* is sheltered with pinewoods. Very clear waters, ideal for all the family. Plenty of restaurants and souvenir shops nearby. Cliffs and woods for walking. Reached by buses from Ibiza town and Santa Eulalia.

Cala Salida North of San Antonio, small sandy beach suitable for children. Reached by car or boat from San Antonio.

Cala Talamanca Sandy beach close to Ibiza town. Hotels, restaurants, sunbeds, pedalos. Popular for all the family but not much shade.

Es Pujols, Formentera lives up to the holiday brochure's description of the resort — sun, sea and sand.

Cala Tarida There are many facilities including sailing and windsurfing. Reached by bus or boat from San Antonio.

Cala San Vicente Deep inlet surrounded by high cliffs, on north east coast. Pebble and sand, can be windy. Good fish restaurants. Reached by bus from Ibiza town and Santa Eulalia,

Cala Vedella On south west coast. Pleasant sandy bay at edge of new *urbanizacion*. Beach bars and restaurant. Pedalos, windsurfing, sub aqua. Reached by boat from San Antonio or by road.

Playa Cavallet Ibiza's official nudist beach. Sand dunes, beach bar, nearby restaurant. Little shade, Reached by road; turn left before the Las Salinas salt works.

Playa D'En Bossa Largest beach with many hotels along edge. Fine white sands, shallow water, sunbeds, beach bars, windsurfing. Reached by bus from Ibiza town.

Play Es Cana Deep natural harbour with sandy beach, pinewoods. Safe for children. Pedalos, water slide, windsurfing, boat trips. Reached by bus and boat from Santa Eulalia.

Playa del Figueral Northeast coast. Narrow sandy beach with rocks. Pedalos, windsurfing and restaurants. Reached by bus from Santa Eulalia.

Playa Las Salinas Clean sands backed by low pinewoods. Nearby restaurant, popular at weekends with Ibicencos. Sunbeds, pedalos, windsurfing. Reached by bus from Ibiza town.

Playa San Miguel Deep natural harbour and sandy beach. Wooded hills for walking. Nearby caves. Shops, bars, hotels. Reached by bus from Ibiza town.

Port D'Es Torrent Semi-circular cove with sandy beach and rocky pool. Interesting for under water swimming. Trees shade hills for walking. Bus and boat from San Antonio.

Formentera

Cala Sahona Small sandy bay on west coast. Quite natural, with low pines. One *hostal*. Reached by bus from La Sabina.

Playa de Mitjorn Long arc of white sand, eight kilometres. Hotels and holiday complex. Part still undeveloped. Seems no problems for naturists, but watch for the effect of the hot sun. Reached by road.

Playa Es Pujols The island's premier resort, sandy beach with rocks, clear shallow water. Sometimes tar on beach. Windsurfing, pedalos, nearby shops, bars and restaurants. Reached by bus from Puerto Sabina — or bicycle!

Ses Salinas Narrow strip of undeveloped sand dunes with beach bars, near La Sabina. Good walk by sea shore towards Moll Morrig. The beaches of Illetas and Levante have been officially set aside for nude sunbathing.

TWO
Getting there

By air

Ibiza's largest modern airport is located eight kilometres to the west of Ibiza town; it serves both domestic and international flights. Always busy, the airport terminal handled 2,512,440 passengers in 1984. Buses link with Ibiza town, a fifteen minute drive away, departing every thirty minutes. There are trolleys available and also porters to carry your luggage (for a small charge) to the many waiting taxis. Cost of a taxi from the airport to Ibiza town is 700 pesetas (£3.18). Pieces of luggage are 15 pesetas each, Sunday and fiestas an extra 30 pesetas, and after 2200 hrs another 25 pesetas. Waiting time is charged at 900 pesetas (£4) an hour.

There is a large car park; charges are 60 pesetas for the first hour, 45 pesetas for subsequent hours with a maximum of 300 pesetas (£1.36) for 24 hours. Inside the airport, a stark building with escalator and lift, you find the usual facilities of toilets (including one for the disabled), tourist information, car rental firms, hotel booking desks and duty free shop. There are telephones, souvenirs and a rather expensive auto service cafeteria. Also available are wheelchairs for those that need them.

At this airport arrival and departure are by announcement only, there are no indicator boards. Iberia Airways has an information desk; the staff speak some English. Tel: 30 03 00. Reservations. Tel: 30 09 54.

There is no airport on Formentera. Visitors may arrive by air at Ibiza airport, then transfer by coach to the ferry port. The crossing to La Sabina (Formentera) takes about one hour.

Scheduled flights
Scheduled flights into and out of Ibiza are run by the following airlines:
- Iberia — London to Ibiza. Four times a week. Flight time 2¼ hrs.
- Iberia & Aviaco — Barcelona to Ibiza. Twice daily. Flight time 45 min.
- Iberia & Aviaco — Palma to Ibiza. Three flights daily. Flight time 30 min.

The cost of the Iberia flight, single, between London and Ibiza, is 37,440 pesetas (£170).

Package flights and tours
The majority of visitors to Ibiza and Formentera arrive on a package holiday flight. These can be arranged by most travel agents in the UK.

Among the tour operators offering package holidays are Aqua Sun, Blue Sky, Carousel, Enterprise, Falcon, Global, Horizon, Intasun, Thomas Cook, Sovereign and Thomson Holidays.

Duty Free Allowance into the UK

300 cigarettes or 75 cigars or 400 grms tobacco.

5 litres of wine.

1½ litres of spirits over 22% or 3 litres below 22%, (e.g. fortified or sparkling wine) or a further 3 litres of wine.

Perfume 90 cc.

Toilet water 375 cc.

Other goods, £250 worth, but no more than 50 litres of beer, or more than 25 mechanical lighters.

Inter island flights
To fly to Menorca from Ibiza it is necessary to change aircraft in Palma, Majorca as there is no direct flight. The single air fare from Ibiza to Palma is 2,865 pesetas (£13). Palma to Menorca is also 2,865 pesetas (£13). There are daily flights. Formentera does not have an airport.

By sea

To visit Ibiza and Formentera by ferry from Europe you will need to depart from one of the following ports: in Spain, from Barcelona, Valencia or Denia (80km south of Valencia); in France, from Sète (Montpellier). Only departures from Barcelona, Valencia and Denia go directly to Ibiza. From Denia there is a ferry that goes directly to Formentera. From France it is necessary to take a ferry to Palma (Majorca) and then to Ibiza or Formentera. Details of these ferry services are given on pages 26 and 27.

By road to ferry ports

Road travel to your ferry port presents little problem, being merely a question of choice of route. But it is essential to book your ferries well in advance during the summer months.

Sealink Ferries operate frequent services throughout the year: Dover to Calais (crossing time 1½ hours); Folkestone to Boulogne (1¾ hours); Newhaven to Dieppe (4 hours). The ships are modern and fast, with easy loading facilities. On board there are bars, restaurants, comfortable cabins, shops and amusements. The non-peak time single fare from Dover to Calais for two persons with car is £58. Reservations can be made in most travel agents or by writing to: Sealink UK Ltd, PO Box 29, London SW1V 1JX. Tel: 01-834 8122.

Route 1 — Calais to Barcelona, Valencia and to Denia (1,794 km)
If you wish to travel quickly by road from the UK, it is suggested that you cross the English Channel from Folkestone or Dover to Boulogne or Calais, then take the Route Nationale 1 to Paris. Join the Periphérique (fast ring road) and follow the sign Est (east), and the signs for Autoroute Sud (south) A6 or Lyon Autoroute A6. Continue on Autoroute, leaving at Orange to join the A9 to Narbonne. From there, follow the coastal route N11 to Barcelona and Valencia, or Autopista A17, and on to Denia, which will be signposted from the route to Alicante.

Route 2 — Plymouth (Devon) via Santander (Northern Spain) to Barcelona, Valencia and Denia (1,103 km)
Brittany Ferries operate a twice weekly vehicle and passenger ferry (from Millbay Docks, Plymouth) throughout the year. The crossing takes twenty-four hours in a fully stabilised ship. Driving into the car deck is a simple operation. The ship is comfortable, with air-conditioned two- and four-berth cabins, some with flowers and

toilets. There are wide promenade and sun decks, lounges with bars and a dance floor, electronic games, duty free shops, cinema and children's room. The single fare including cabin from Plymouth to Santander for two persons and car is between £180 and £259.

Santander to Barcelona is around 625 km. One can join the toll motorway (*autopista peaje*) at Bilbao which goes right past Zaragoza to Barcelona. There are frequent service areas, some are not open twenty-four hours but ample notice is given of this. It is a quiet and pleasant motorway, the toll costing about £15 from Bilbao to Barcelona.

Santander to Valencia by the shortest route (739 km) is through Burgos and Madrid. There is no motorway and quite a stiff climb to Burgos over the Puerto de Escudo (1,011 m). This route is not ideal if you are travelling between November and April because of snow. If motorway driving is preferred take the route from Santander via Zaragoza to Barcelona (described above) and thence to Valencia, which would make the distance 1,023 km.

Santander to Denia is around 751 km. Follow the route from Santander to Valencia already outlined, then take the coast road towards Alicante and after about 50 km turn off for Denia.

Route 3 — Calais to Sète (1,100 km)
Should you wish to travel via Sète (near Montpelier), then take the French motorway system (A26, A1, A3, A6 and A7) which bypasses Paris and Lyon. It is a toll motorway with service areas about every thirty kilometres. This is about a 12-hour drive. Remember that the Sète to Ibiza ferry operates only from mid-June to mid-September, and that it is necessary to take a further ferry from Ibiza to Formentera.

Ferries from Spain
The **Trasmediterranea Shipping Company** run a regular vehicle and passenger service from mainland Spain to the Balearic Islands. An inter island service is operated throughout the year, but there is no ferry that goes directly from Ibiza to Menorca; it is necessary to travel via Majorca (see page 29). All Trasmediterranea ferries are drive on and off, from either the stern or the side of the ship. Sometimes it is necessary to reverse your vehicle through the car deck, and this is generally carried out with assistance from the ship's crew. Services are:
- Barcelona to Ibiza. Four times a week. A 9½ hour voyage. During Easter and from 16 June to 14 September there is a daily service. On occasions the ferry goes via Palma, making it a 15-hour voyage.

- Valencia to Ibiza. Twice weekly. A 6-hour voyage. During Easter and from 16 June to 14 September the service is increased to four times a week.

The UK agents for Trasmediterranea are at present Melia Travel, 12 Dover Street, London W1X 4NS. Tel: 01-499 6731. Approximate cost of the single fare from either Barcelona or Valencia to Ibiza for two adults with car is £126. The approximate cost for the single fare for one adult without car and excluding cabin is £18.

There is a daily vehicle and passenger ferry service from Ibiza port to Formentera.

Ferry reservations can be made in Spain through travel agents. The Trasmediterranea Shipping Company have offices in the major towns and ports in Spain. Head Office — Plaza Manuel Gómez Moreno, Edificio Bronce, Apartado de Correos 982, Madrid 20. At operating ports — Via Payetana 2, Barcelona; Avenida Manuel Soto Ing 15, Valencia; Muelle Viejo 5, Palma, Majorca; Avenida Bartolomé Vincente Ramón, Ibiza. Tel: 30 37 66.

During the summer months **Flebasa Lines** run a frequent vehicle and passenger service from Denia, near Alicante, Spain to Puerto San Antonio, Ibiza. The voyage takes three hours. The ships are modern and vehicles drive on and off. There is a coach service to convey passengers from the bus stations in Valencia and Alicante to the ferry at Denia. The approximate cost of the single fare from Denia to Ibiza for two adults is £18, which includes coach service from Valenica or Alicante if required. Reservations can be made in Spain through travel agents or at the ports of Denia and Puerto San Antonio.

Ferries from France

Trasmediterranea operate a return vehicle and passenger ferry service from Sète (near Montpellier) to Valencia, calling at Palma (Majorca) and Ibiza. The service operates from mid-June to mid-September.

- Sète to Ibiza. Tuesday and Saturday, leaving 1600 hrs and arriving the following day at 1400 hrs.
- Ibiza to Sète. Monday and Friday, leaving at 1000 hrs and arriving at 0900 hrs the following day.

The approximate cost of the single fare, Sète to Ibiza, for two adults with car is 36,630 pesetas (£166.30).

Reservations can be made through UK agents, Melia Travel (12 Dover Street, London, W1X 2NS. Tel: 01-499 6731) and through the SNCM agent in Sète (4 Quai d'Alger. Tel: 74 70 55).

There is a daily vehicle and passenger ferry service from Ibiza port to Formentera.

On the sea approach to Ibiza one sees the old city and cathedral standing imposingly against the clear sky.

Inter island ferries

The Trasmediterranea Shipping Company operate a vehicle and passenger ferry service from Palma, Majorca to Ibiza and Menorca. From Majorca, Ibiza and Menorca there are services to Valencia and Barcelona.

- Ibiza to Palma. Twice weekly. A 4½-hour voyage.
- Palma to Menorca. Once a week. A 6½-hour voyage.

The approximate cost of the single fare, excluding cabin, from Ibiza to Palma for two adults with car is £62. The fare is the same between Palma and Menorca.

Umafisa is the name of the vehicle and passenger ferry that operates frequent daily sailings between Ibiza town and the island of Formentera (less frequent in the low season). The ship is small but modern and comfortable and the voyage takes one hour. The fare for one adult is 385 pesetas (£1.75) and vehicle 1,500 pesetas (£6.80), single. There are other small passenger ferries plying from Ibiza, San Antonio and Santa Eulalia to Formentera.

The arrival of ferry ships into Ibiza town port causes much interest for passengers and people ashore.

By rail and ferry

Rail tickets for travel from London to Barcelona (where the Trasmediterannea ferry can be taken to Ibiza — thence a further ferry from Ibiza to Formentera) are obtained from principal British Rail stations, travel agents and Sealink Travel Ltd., Continental Travel Centre, Liverpool Station, London, EC2.

This example gives an idea of how the journey will go — but be sure to check current timetables carefully before setting out.

Day 1	London Victoria		train dep.	14.30h
	Dover		ferry dep.	1630h
	Calais (France)	train no. 10400	dep.	1940h
Day 2	Port Bou (France/Spain border)		arr.	1105h
	Barcelona (Spain)		arr.	1445h
	Barcelona to Ibiza		ferry dep.	2330h
Day 3	Ibiza		arr.	0930h

Fares from London to Barcelona are Adult 2nd Class single £88.90, return £148; Senior Citizen return £96.

By coach and ferry

There are a number of coach services from London to Spain that pass through Barcelona. From **April to September** Euroways run a service that includes the ferry from Barcelona to Ibiza. (A further ferry travels from Ibiza to Formentera.)

The inclusive fare quoted is £66 single and £123 return; this includes an armchair on the ferry, which is a night crossing.

Coaches depart from London on a Monday, Wednesday and Friday. The example gives an idea of how the journey will go — but be sure to check current timetables carefully before setting out.

Day 1	London Victoria	coach dep.	1000h
	Dover	arr.	12.30h
Day 2	Barcelona	arr.	1245h
	Barcelona to Ibiza	ferry dep.	2330h
Day 3	Ibiza	arr.	0700h

Reservations can be made through travel agents or Euroways main office (52 Grosvenor Gardens, Victoria, London SW1. Tel: 01-730 3433).

Yacht club facilities

There are two yacht clubs in Ibiza port, one in San Antonio and a further one in the process of being built at Santa Eulalia. In Formentera there is one yacht club in the port at La Sabina. Facilities are listed below.

Club Náutico Ibiza 1km from Ibiza town. Tel: 30 11 35. Berths with water and electricity, telephones, slipway, sailing school, water sports club.
Puerto Deportivo Ibiza Nueva Maritimo, Ibiza town. Tel: 30 01 18. Berths with water and electricity, weather reports, fuel, telephones, slipway, repairs, chandler, water sports club.
Puerto de Cala Sabina Formentera. Berths with water and electricity, fuel, crane, slipway, repairs, water sports club.

Daily mooring fees range from 660 pesetas (£3) for craft up to 10 tons to 885 pesetas (£4) for 15 to 20 tons, per day.

Yacht clubs welcome visiting craft; further information can be had from the club secretaries. There is also a useful handbook giving information on yacht clubs in Spain, *Guia Nautico Turistica de España* published by the Ministry of Tourism, 750 pesetas (£3.40).

THREE

Where to stay

Accommodation in Ibiza and Formentera ranges from four-star hotels to self-catering apartments and simple guest houses. Tourist hotels and resorts are spread round the coast, usually close to a sandy beach. The inland villages have only simple facilities.

The hotel season is confined largely to the period April to the end of September or October, the most popular months being July and August. In Ibiza, San Antonio in the west is the liveliest resort, with Santa Eulalia gaining in polularity. The largest beach is at Playa D'en Bossa in the south. There is plenty to do in Es Cana, where boat excursions make a change from the beach. For a quieter holiday choose Portinatx on the north east corner of Ibiza, and if you really want to get away to the mountains then Playa San Miguel will provide cliff scenery, good walks, an interesting cave and comfortable hotels.

Formentera has one four-star hotel, one three-star, one one-star and eight two-star hotel apartments. There are also 21 one-star *hostales,* which are really guesthouses.

There are three holiday villages, Punta Arabi, Santa Eulalia, Ibiza. Tel: 33 00 85. Ciudad Mar, Portínatx, Ibiza. Tel: 33 30 77. Punta Prima, Formentera. Tel: 32 03 68. A full list of accommodation can be obtained from the Oficina de Informacion y Turismo, Vara de Rey 13, Ibiza. Tel: 30 19 00.

The star rating

The star rating system gives you an idea of what to expect for your money.

Four-star hotel Air conditioning in public rooms and bedrooms. Seventy-five per cent of rooms have a full bathroom; twenty-five per cent have shower, washbasin, WC. Telephone, laundry and ironing service. Garage, lift and bar.

Three-star hotel Permanently installed heating. Fifty per cent of rooms have a full bathroom. Fifty per cent have shower, washbasin, WC. Telephone, laundry and ironing service. Lift and bar.

Two-star hotel. Permanently installed heating. Fifteen per cent of rooms have a full bathroom, forty-seven per cent have shower, washbasin, WC. One common bathroom to six bedrooms. Telephone, laundry and ironing service. Lift in buildings of more than four storeys.

One-star hotel Permanently installed heating. Twenty-five per cent of rooms have washbasin, shower and WC; twenty-five per cent have washbasin and shower. One common bathroom to every seven bedrooms. Telephone, laundry and ironing service. Lift in buildings of more than five storeys.

Three-star guesthouse Five per cent of rooms have full bathroom; ten per cent have shower, washbasin and WC. One common bathroom to every eight rooms. Telephone, laundry and ironing service. Lift.

Two-star guesthouse All rooms have washbasin. One common bathroom to every ten rooms. Telephone. Lift in five storey buildings.

One-star guesthouse All rooms have washbasin with cold water. One common bathroom to twelve rooms. Telephone.

A selection of hotels and guesthouses

This small selection of hotels is listed alphabetically under star rating and is not meant to be exhaustive. There are many other good hotels on the islands. Prices quoted are for privately arranged accommodation (non-package tour).

Ibiza

Hotel Los Molinos (four star) Figueretas, Ibiza. Tel: 30 22 50. Open all year round. 147 rooms, all with bathroom, most with terrace and sea view. Totally air conditioned and centrally heated. This well appointed hotel with a quiet Spanish atmosphere is situated on a rocky peninsula at the western edge of Ibiza town and below the old city walls. It takes about twenty minutes to walk to the centre. A small manmade sandy beach and two swimming pools, one for young children, have surrounding sub tropical gardens that include a thousand year old olive tree. The hotel has a conference room for

150 persons and is used by business people. Double room with seaview, per night, 6,100 pesetas (£27.72) to 9,800 pesetas (£44.54). Breakfast 450 pesetas (£2). Lunch or dinner 1,800 (£8.18).

Hotel Palmyra (four-star) San Antonio, Ibiza. Tel: 34 03 54. 160 rooms, all with bathroom and terrace. Double room per night 10,890 pesetas (£49.50). Breakfast 700 pesetas (£3.18). Lunch or dinner 1,850 pesetas (£8.40). Air conditioning in bars, lounges and restaurant. This is a luxurious and very comfortable hotel, having a well established reputation for a high standard of service. The decor is gracious and restful, with the staff quietly attentive. It is within walking distance of the centre of town. This hotel has dancing every night, a bridge room and conference hall. You are expected to dress for dinner; there is full waiter service except for breakfast, which is a buffet. Outside a palm shaded patio has a large swimming pool and layout chairs; during the summer months buffet luncheons are served here. Reached by a few steps is a small private sandy beach which has a splendid view of the beautiful Bahia de San Antonio. The hotel belongs to the Fiesta Group.

Hotel Hacienda (four-star) San Miguel, Ibiza. Tel: 33 30 46. 56 rooms. Double room with breakfast per night 4,750 pesetas (£21.60) to 7,650 pesetas (£34.77). Lunch or dinner 2,500 pesetas (£11.36). Buffet barbecue 3,000 pesetas (£13.63). Hidden away on top of a mountain in the north, this small and exclusive hotel is built, as the name implies, in Spanish *hacienda* style; the low white building has an inner courtyard that contains a swimming pool, attractively floodlit at night, patios and sun terraces. Tastefully furnished bedrooms have verandahs overlooking delightful gardens and cliff top scenery. Buffet luncheons are served by the pool and some nights there is dancing. These utterly peaceful surroundings make a romantic setting for a honeymoon. To explore the rest of the island it is necessary to have a car. Puerto San Miguel is over three kilometres away.

Hotel Pinet Playa (three star) San Antonio, Ibiza. Tel: 34 02 50. 291 rooms. Double room per night 1,500 pesetas (£6.80) to 5,100 pesetas (£23). Breakfast 400 pesetas (£1.80). Lunch or dinner 900 pesetas (£4). Air conditioned restaurant, bar and lounges. Situated three kilometres from San Antonio on the Punta Pinet Beach, this is one of the largest hotels in Ibiza and one of the few that remain open until the end of November. A member of the CHM Hotel group (British Caledonian) it offers good value for family holidays. Children love this hotel because of the special programmes arranged for their entertainment. The adult's and children's swimming pools are heated in winter. Video films in English, dancing, discothèque and a card room are amongst the facilities. It is self-service for the first two courses at lunch and dinner and there is a weekly candle lit dinner.

Hotel Los Loros (three star) Santa Eulalia, Ibiza. Tel: 33 07 61. 262 rooms. Double room per night 6,000 pesetas (£27.27). Breakfast 350 pesetas (£1.59). Lunch or dinner 1,600 pesetas (£7.27). Belonging to the well known group of Sol Hotels, the large and modern Los Loros is located on the eastern outskirts of Santa Eulalia, near pinewoods, with good views overlooking the Mediterranean. Although there is no sandy beach you can bathe off the rocks and in the outdoor and indoor swimming pools. The hotel has a lively entertainments and sports programme; there is dancing and a separate disco. Special attention is given to families with young children; high chairs and cots are provided and early suppers can be requested. All meals are help-yourself buffets. The choice is very good and varied, with a generous selection at breakfast time. This is a good family hotel with a cheery atmosphere. Coach excursions are arranged and cars and bicycles can be hired.

Hotel Goleta (three star) Play D'en Bossa, Ibiza. Tel: 30 21 58. 252 rooms. Double room, 4,500 pesetas (£20.45) to 5,500 pesetas (£25) per night. Breakfast 350 pesetas (£1.60). Lunch or dinner 1,200 pesetas (£5.50). This friendly Ibizan owned hotel and its sister, **Tres Carabelas,** are just two kilometres from Ibiza town. Both are 'fun for all the family' with plenty of sports and entertainments arranged. All bedrooms have bathroom, telephone, heating and a sea view terrace. There are several bars, disco, ballroom and hairdresser. Holidaymakers can enjoy the facilities of both hotels. The large white sandy beach of Playa D'en Bossa is a short walk away.

Hotel Galéon (three star) Puerto San Miguel, Ibiza. Tel: 33 30 19. 182 bedrooms all with seaview balconies. Double room per night from 2,685 pesetas (£12.20) to 4,380 pesetas (£19.90). Breakfast 360 pesetas (£1.63). Lunch or dinner 940 pesetas (£4.27). This modern hotel is in a picturesque and a quiet position on a cliffside in the north, overlooking Puerto San Miguel. The locally born staff and head waiter give a friendly welcome to all their guests and go out of their way to be helpful. There is free *sangría* served on one night of your stay. The outdoor swimming pool has plenty of room for sunbathing. Puerto San Miguel has a sandy beach with pedalos for hire, a beach bar and restaurants. However, to reach the beach it is necessary to climb down many steps or drive, a consideration if taking young children or disabled persons. The Cave de Can Marca is within walking distance of the hotel and the surrounding pinewoods are interesting to explore.

Hotel Panorama (three star) Playa Es Cana, Ibiza. Tel: 30 00 00. 137 rooms. Double room per night from 2,500 pesetas (£11.36) to 3,800 pesetas (£17.27). Breakfast 350 pesetas (£1.60). Lunch or dinner 1,250 pesetas (£5.68). Built on the seafront in the wide bay of Es Cana, this hotel, one of the Med Playa group, is noted for its relaxed atmosphere, helpful manager, cheerful waitresses and excellent chef. Many guests return again and again. Es Cana has a gently sloping beach making it safe for children. There are supermarkets, tourist shops and restaurants in this small resort. Daily boat trips visit nearby islets and there is a bus and ferry service to Santa Eulalia, about five kilometres to the south.

Hotel Piscus Park (two star) San Antonio, Ibiza. Tel: 34 06 50. 366 rooms all with bathroom and balcony. Double room from 2,550 pesetas (£11.60) to 3,000 pesetas (£13.64). Breakfast 315 pesetas (£1.43). Lunch or Dinner 1,500 pesetas (£6.82). This large, modern hotel is for fun loving people who want to be in the centre of things, and is not the place for those seeking peace and quiet. It is situated right on the main road in the centre of town. The Extasis, one of the resort's most popular discos, is quite close and stays open until the early hours. The hotel is a useful location for getting buses and ferries to other parts of Ibiza, being just across the road from the promenade.

Hostal La Marina (one star) Ibiza town. Tel: 30 14 50. Double room per night from 1,500 pesetas (£6.82) to 1,700 pesetas (£7.73). Breakfast 200 pesetas (£0.90). Lunch or dinner 800 pesetas (£3.64). Located along the port in the fishermen's old quarter, this building has been a guesthouse for 128 years and is full of local atmosphere. Many of the tables and chairs seen in the restaurant are genuine antiques, as is the sideboard and aged clock. Bedrooms are simply furnished and have a washbasin and hot water. The modern bathroom is along the corridor. It is suggested that valuables are securely locked up. This is a useful base for anyone wishing to enjoy the nightlife of Ibiza town.

Hostal Galfi (one star) San Antonio, Ibiza. Tel: 34 09 12. Double room 1,950 pesetas (£8.86). Breakfast 250 pesetas (£1.14). This small and friendly guesthouse is located about a kilometre from San Antonio. If you wish to get to know Ibizan hoteliers, then you will enjoy talking to owner-managers Marlies and Luis Hormigo in this friendly holiday spot. A small swimming pool is set in a pretty garden of green tropical shrubs. Entertainment consists of TV, video English films, chess and darts. There is a bus service to the sandy beach of Port des Torrent and San Antonio.

Hotel Mare Nostrum (one star) Playa D'en Bossa, Ibiza. Tel: 30 26 52. 528 rooms. Double room per night 2,900 pesetas (£13.18) to 3,100 pesetas (£14). Breakfast 300 pesetas (£1.36). Lunch or dinner 950 pesetas (£4.32). Officially listed by the Spanish Tourist Office as one star, the Thomson Summer Sun Brochure rates it two stars. One of the largest hotels in Ibiza, it is always busy. This hotel is excellent for families who want to enjoy themselves and have plenty of cheerful fun and few restrictions. Everything is very informal and all meals are self-service buffet. Entertainment includes TV, video English films, dancing, fancy dress and special games for children and grandmothers. The hotel's large swimming pool has a section for children. There is a bus stop nearby for getting to Ibiza town and a sandy beach is a few yards across the road.

Hotel Residencia Ca's Catalá (HR) Santa Eulalia, Ibiza. Tel: 33 10 06. 12 rooms all with shower or bathroom. Double room including breakfast per night 4,700 pesetas (£21.36). Situated within walking distance of the town and beach, this small, quiet English-owned hotel, once a private house, has individually decorated bedrooms. The airy dining room overlooks an attractive and colourful garden, where the swimming pool and layout chairs are ideal for relaxing. Inside there are two sitting rooms and a bar, cool in summer and heated when necessary. Arrangements can be made to pick up guests from the airport.

Formentera

Hotel La Mola (four star) Playa Mitjorn, Formentera. Tel: 32 00 50. Open from 15 May to 31 October. 328 rooms (262 in main building, 66 in bungalows). Double room per night 7,500 pesetas (£34) to 9,700 pesetas (£44). Breakfast 500 pesetas (£2.27). Lunch or dinner 1,300 pesetas (£5.90). A luxurious hotel at the end of a superb white sandy beach, this is the place to get your overall suntan and indulge yourself with good food and disco dancing. A wide range of sports include the very popular windsurfing but if you play tennis you will need your own equipment. The three restaurants are air conditioned and there is a special menu for children and *à la carte*.

Hotel Formentera Playa (three star) Playa Mitjorn, Formentera. Tel: 32 00 00. Open from 1 April to 31 October. 211 bedrooms all with bathroom and verandah. Double room per night from 3,100 pesetas (£14) to 5,100 pesetas (£23). Breakfast 325 pesetas (£1.48). Lunch or dinner 1,025 pesetas (£4.66). Built right by the beach, this family hotel is for people who like to relax on the sands or by the pool, but do not expect too much entertainment. However, there is disco dancing three times a week and TV in the lounge. Two tennis courts have equipment for hire, a volley ball court, crazy golf and table tennis provide for sport. Plenty of opportunity for swimming, sunbathing and walking among sweet scented pine trees. Meals are self service buffet and there is a beach bar.

Hostal Cala Sahona (two star) Cala Sahona, Formentera. Tel: 32 00 30. 69 rooms. Double room with bathroom from 2,235 pesetas (£10) to 3,165 pesetas (£14.40) per night; without bath but with toilet from 1,925 pesetas (£8.75) to 2,525 pesetas (£11.70). Breakfast 195 (£0.89). Lunch or dinner 605 pesetas (£2.75). Ideal for a beach holiday this small guesthouse is tucked away in a very secluded position on the west coast, close to the sands and pine woods of Cala Sahona. Juan Ferrer's family own and manage this friendly *hostal* and the whole ambience is quiet and restful — a real 'get away from it all' place. The swimming pool has a children's section. Babies' cots are available. The capital, San Francisco Javier is just six kilometres away.

This large sandy beach at Cala Llonga has plenty of space for ball games but can become very hot in the summer.

Apartments and villas

Self catering accommodation is becoming more popular in Ibiza and Formentera, and new *urbanizaciónes* (modern villages) are being built. These purpose-built areas are usually quite self-contained, with supermarkets, hairdressers, bars, restaurants, shops, sports centres, discos, boat storage and car parks. Basic equipment in apartments will include bed linen, towels, kitchen equipment, cooking facilities, crockery, cutlery and glasses. Most have maid service and if there is a garden it is tended. A central reception will have information on display and offer excursion bookings and currency exchange facilities.

Package holidays

There are many firms operating holidays to Ibiza and Formentera. These provide a wide choice and offer good value to holidaymakers with limited time. They allow customers to budget in advance for most of their holiday expenses.

When you book a package holiday the air fare is included, plus transport to and from your destination in Ibiza or Formentera, unless otherwise stated. Tour operators' brochures will give details of flight arrangements, type of resort, entertainments and star rating of accommodation. This will vary from four-star hotels to modest guesthouses and self-catering apartments. For a list of package holiday firms see page 24.

On arrival at the airport in Ibiza, you will be met by the representative of your tour operator. He or she will show you to the coach which will take you to your hotel or apartment. The next day you meet the courier again at a welcoming party where you are informed of local interests, excursions and entertainments. It is advisable to seek the assistance of the courier who should know the hotel and islands well and is there to make your stay enjoyable. These hard-working representatives are usually kind and patient; they also have a sense of humour!

> 'Remember, that if thou hadst been created to stay in one place, thou wouldst have been given roots!
>
> Remember, when in a foreign country, thou shalt be prepared to eat somewhat as the locals do!
>
> Thou shalt not expect to find things as they are at home, for thou has left home to find things new!'

This is an extract from the couriers' *Ten Commandments for a Happy Holiday*.

Camping and motorcaravanning

Camping rules that apply in mainland Spain also apply to Ibiza. A copy of the camping regulations for Spain should be obtained from the Spanish National Tourist Office, (57/58 St James's Street, London SW1A LD. Tel: 01 499 0901). Camping is not allowed in Formentera and there are no campsites.

It is necessary to have a Camping Carnet, but it is an advantage especially for those who camp outside official sites, as third party insurance is included. Camping Carnets can be obtained from camping organisations such as the AA, RAC and the Caravan Club and cost £1.50. A passport size photograph is required.

While en route you may find that amongst the several campsites near Barcelona, **Camping International Barcino** is very convenient for visiting the city, being on a bus route to the centre and the port where the ferry leaves for Ibiza. But during the high season the camp can become very crowded and dusty, so best regard it only as a transit site. Street parking of unattended camping vehicles in Barcelona is to be avoided.

On Ibiza there are four campsites open from April. Approximate campsite charges for one night at these sites are 180 pesetas (£0.80) per tent, 150 pesetas (0.68) per person.

Camping Garbi (Class 1a) Open April to September. Situated at Playa D'en Bossa, this is the best of the sites, with capacity for 250 persons, tents, caravans and motorcaravans are allowed. Amongst the facilities are electric hook ups, childrens playground and a supermarket stocking camping Gaz.

Camping Cala Bassa (Class 2a) Open April to October. This site is situated on the outskirts of Cala Bassa. There are directions down an unmade road for three kilometres. It is licensed to take 400 persons some of which are in static caravans. As well as a supermarket there is a bar/restaurant and electric hook-ups.

Camping San Antonio (Class 2) Open April to September. At km14 on the Ibiza town to San Antonio road. Another large camp which can take 274 persons, Being close to the town and on a bus route it is convenient for excursions. It also has shelter from the hot sunshine under tall palm and pine trees. Nearby are orange groves and market gardens. There is a bar and Camping Gaz is stocked.

Camping Florida (Class 3a) Open April to October. This site is located between Santa Eulalia and Es Cana, right on the coast with a sandy beach. It takes 300 persons. The pitches are level and under pine trees that give welcome shade. The pleasant bar has TV and serves meals. Camping Gaz and electric hook-ups are available.

Speaking generally, Ibiza's camp sites have been somewhat neglected compared with mainland Spain. This may be because they have attracted the 'hippy' type of camper in the past. Now that this is no longer such a problem it is hoped the situation will improve.

Further details of these camping places can be obtained from the Tourist Office in Ibiza town.

During spring, summer and autumn Ibiza is a pleasant island to tour with a motorcaravan. By using one of the campsites as a base, day trips to towns, villages and beaches will be interesting and varied. The northern part has quiet roads that make driving leisurely and there are plenty of wayside bars and restaurants if you wish to treat yourself to a meal. The country folk are polite and gentle and will respond if you give them a wave of greeting.

On the Trasmediterranea ferry charges for motorcaravans are the same as for cars, which is determined by length. A vehicle between 4.5 and 6m long costs 12,700 pesetas (£57) single fare Barcelona to Ibiza. If you do not require a cabin you can book a *butaca turista,* which is like a reclining aircraft seat. This costs 4,080 pesetas (£18) single, per person. For other ferry details see Chapter 2.

Camping off site

It is possible to free park with a motorcaravan on Ibiza but it is not encouraged by the authorities. Overnight parking is allowed at the airport car park. Motorcaravans have been known to park in quiet places, like outside country bars or near a beach. At all times it is necessary to be vigilant and to get permission from the owner of the land. Note that all forms of camping are prohibited on Formentera.

Taking children to Ibiza and Formentera

Children of all ages will enjoy being in Ibiza and Formentera, if you take care to select a hotel or apartment which provides for their amusement. There are a few hotels where young children would disturb the other visitors but this should be apparent on reading the package tour brochure, as these always refer to facilities for children. The Ibicencos are fond of children and spend a lot of time looking after them, so they will be pleased to see visitors with the same attitude.

Modern hotels and apartments generally provide cots and high chairs for infants. Play rooms, paddling pool and baby sitting services (charges are about 400 pesetas (£1.80) per hour) help to make life easier for parents with very small children. Toys and

The translucent waters of Cala San Vicente, seen here from the surrounding pine clad hills.

things for the beach, including warm weather clothing, can be found in supermarkets and shops. Note that baby food is available in *farmacías* (chemists) and not generally in supermarkets. Toilet requisites are to be had in *droguerias* rather than in *farmacias*.

Some package tour operators offer hotels that specialise in catering for families with youngsters, there you will find staff trained to look after children and run Mini Clubs with programmes designed to amuse and entertain their young members. Badges are issued, competitions organised and outings arranged. This allows parents some relaxation from their responsibilities and time to follow their own pursuits.

Young children are allowed in bars, cafés, restaurants, and hotel lounges until very late at night and even on to the dance floor. It is worth remembering not to let them become over tired. An afternoon or early evening rest is sensible; even if they protest it is worth being firm to keep the child from getting exhausted, and perhaps misbehaving as a result.

Care should be taken, even with teenagers, that they do not have too much sunshine, especially during the first few days. With the excitement of the change of surroundings and different foods, it is easy to be over indulgent. It is sensible to drink the bottled water (sold in hotels and supermarkets) and to wash well all salads and fruit before eating. However nice that bunch of grapes looks on the market stall do not be tempted to eat without washing them.

In Ibiza and Formentera there are a few public amusement places. However, children will enjoy the many boat excursions and watersports centres. Visits to the **Cova Santa** caves in Ibiza and the **Xeroni Caves** in Formentera provide a wonderful experience; the amazing formations of stalagmites and stalactites illuminated in different colours, are a fairy tale land. But do reassure your children when going in the dark, maybe a small torch would be a good idea.

Another fun thing to do is visit the **Camel Cellar.** There you will have your photograph taken beside two tethered and muzzled camels before you are invited to a wine and liqueur tasting *bodega* cellar. However, watch your children for, although the glasses are very small, mixing drinks can upset the tummy, especially if driving in the hot sunshine afterwards. A sure favourite with youngsters is the **Donkey Trek,** an excursion into the countryside and a barbecue — a great laugh for all the family.

Young children can go on coach excursions and most have a happy time. But remember to take some toys and games for the little ones who do not want to look at scenery for long. When the coach stops be sure to use the toilets, for it is not always possible for the driver to make other stops, especially on narrow and winding roads.

For the older children there are bicycles to hire and land and sea sports to enjoy. Video games, discos, boutiques, hairdressing salons and jewellery shops will lure the pesetas from the pocket of the teenager. By far the greatest attraction will be the lovely sandy beaches and the clear warm sea water. From the beaches listed on page 20, safe swimming can be expected; however, watch out to see the colour of the flag that is flying on the beach. Red means danger, yellow bathe with caution and green safe to bathe. Never take a risk, Please do not force any child into the sea, it is so easy to make them afraid. Use a little encouragement by sitting at the edge of the water, or just paddling. Make a sand castle, then ask for a bucket of water, this will do a lot to gain the child's confidence. Be sure to provide a sun hat and some sun protection cream; even if it seems overcast, the rays of the sun penetrate the clouds and can cause distress to a tender skin.

Should you be unfortunate enough to become separated from your child, call upon the assistance of the hotel reception or the local police (Guardia Civil).

Travel agent services

There are a number of travel agents *(viajes)* in Ibiza town and in the tourist areas of San Antonio and Santa Eulalia. They vary in the services offered, being agents for hotels, apartments, ferries and flight bookings, car rental, coach excursions and currency exchange. Usually opening hours are from 0930 to 1330 hrs and 1630 to 1930 hrs; closed Saturday afternoons, Sunday and on public holidays. They will make travel and accommodation arrangements for those wishing to visit Formentera.

Established firms such as Ultramar Express, Melia, Wagonlits Cook, Barcelo and Cresta have agencies, usually with English speaking representatives. Ultramar Express, Cresta and Melia run excursions in Ibiza and to Formentera in coaches that are modern and comfortable. Some of the principal travel agents in Ibiza are:
— Barcelo, C'an Escandell, Ibiza town. Tel: 30 12 54
— Cresta, Abad y Lasierra, Ibiza town. Tel: 30 32 08
— Melia, Vara de Rey 7, Ibiza town. Tel: 30 39 00
— Ultramar Express, Ignacio Wallis 29, Ibiza town. Tel: 30 35 48
— Wagonlits Cook, Vara de Rey 3, Ibiza town. Tel: 30 13 92
— Intersol, Avenida Generalissimo s/n, Edificio Cruz del Sur, Santa Eulalia. Tel: 30 01 61
— Martour S.A., Miramar 7, San Antonio. Tel: 34 02 94

Property purchase

Ibiza and Formentera present appealing locations for purchasers to invest in property; a number of British have owned property there for a long time.

It is advisable always to get specialist advice on the subject. Selling apartments, bungalows and villas, the administration of property, letting, legal advice, repairs, technical services and insurance are all transactions carried out by real estate companies in Ibiza, Formentera and the UK. Some of the firms employ English-speaking staff to assist clients.

Two estate agents dealing with the above-mentioned transactions are:

Immobiliaria Ibiza Paseo Vara Rey, Ibiza town. Tel: 31 03 00.
Construcentro S.A. Avenida General Franco 2, Santa Eulalia, Ibiza. Tel: 33 09 35.

Pets

If you wish to take your cat or dog with you to Ibiza or Formentera, a Health and Rabies inoculation certificate is required. This has to be stamped by the Spanish Consulate in your own country. Of course, on returning to the UK, your pet will have to spend six months in quarantine.

Veterinary services are provided by martin A Real Del Barco, Garcia Fernandez, Avenida General Franco 3, Santa Eulalia, Ibiza. Tel: 33 08 39. There is a Kennels and Dog Training Centre at C'an Jundal. Km8, Ibiza to San Antonio road. Pet food can be obtained from Supermarkets.

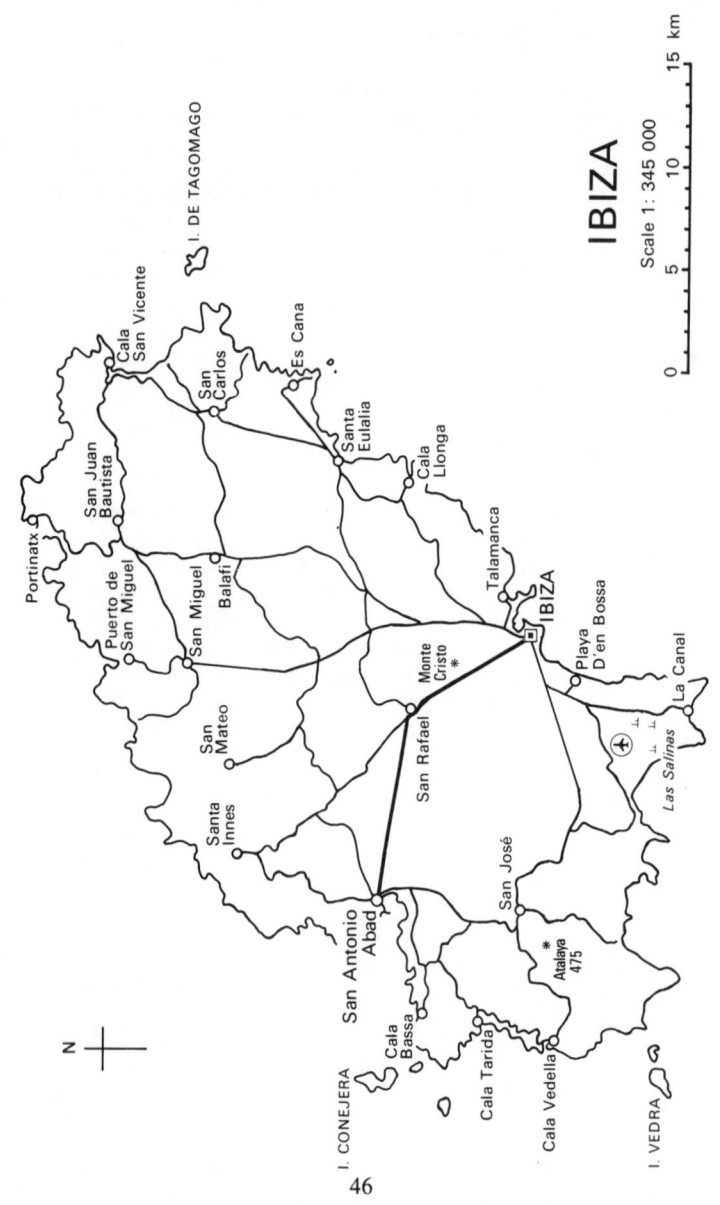

FOUR

Getting about the islands

Roads

The roads on Ibiza and Formentera are not very good, with the exception of the fast new Ibiza to San Antonio motorway and, on Formentera, the road from La Sabina port to San Francisco Javier. The rest suffer from lack of maintenance, very few having proper edges or pavements; indeed a lot have potholes and deep ditches or sandy surfaces on either side.

Fortunately, except in the vicinity of Ibiza town, the roads are reasonably quiet and in the north you can travel for kilometres without seeing another vehicle — though you may see the occasional donkey.

Parking in the main towns of San Antonio, Santa Eulalia and Ibiza town is not easy. The Tráfico Policio will tow away and impound an illegally parked vehicle. The pound is behind Avenida Isidoro Macabich. Heavy yellow metal clamps called *cepos* are put on a rear wheel. A fine must be paid before you can retrieve your vehicle — and there is a very long wait.

It is helpful to have a map when touring by car. Recommended are the maps published by Firestone Hispania, Nos. E54 and T26, obtainable at petrol filling stations and bookshops in Ibiza, or from the UK agent Roger Lascelles (Dept. Firestone), 47 York Road, Brentford, Middlesex, TW8 0PO. Tel: 01-847 0935. Price £2.50.

Rules and recommendations for drivers

If you are taking a car to Menorca and driving through Spain to take the car ferry from either Barcelona or Valencia, you will require the following:

1. International Driving Permit, which must always be carried.
2. International Insurance (Green Card). Your insurance company issues this.
3. Bail Bond (from AA, RAC or insurance company), an indemnity if you are involved in an accident.
4. Vehicle Registration Document.
5. Passport plus photocopy kept separate.
6. Spare set of car light bulbs (Spanish Law Requirement.
7. A red triangle, for warning of breakdown obstruction.
8. Means of changing direction of headlight dip.
9. GB sticker.

Up-to-date information on these subjects is best obtained from the AA, RAC or the Spanish Tourist Office, however the following points are worthy of note:
- Drive on the right hand side of the road.
- Sound your horn when overtaking.
- Stop for pedestrians on crossings.
- Wear seat belts. Police may impose a fine of 1,000 pesetas (£4.54) on the spot if this law is broken.
- Sidelights only are required in built up areas.
- Do not cross the single white line; it is equivalent to our double white line.
- Observe 'no overtaking' signs and speed limits.
- Maximum speed in built up areas is 40 km.p.h.
- Give way to traffic coming from the *right,* especially at roundabouts.
- Motorcyclists must wear crash helmets and travel with lights on.

Car servicing and repairs

There are a number of places for the servicing and repair of cars. Ibiza town has agents for most well known British and foreign makes. There could be a delay in obtaining a particular spare part required from abroad. In country towns a small workshop (*taller mechanico*), which deals with local vehicles, will assist. The standard is good and repairs are promptly effected. Cost will usually be more reasonable than in the UK. Facilities for tyre fitting, battery charging and car washing are available.

Road signs

Most road signs are international. One important traffic control is the direction change (*cambio de sentido*), generally controlled by traffic lights; this prevents vehicles turning across oncoming traffic or from doing a U-turn. Here are some road sign translations:

Aduana	Customs post
Aparcamiento	Parking
Atención	Caution
Blandones	Soft verges
Cedo el paso	Give way
Despacio	Slow
Desvio	Diversion
Derecha	Right
Escuela	School
Estacionamiento prohibido	No parking
Izquierda	Left
Obras	Workmen
Pare, Parada	Stop
Peligro	Danger
Peligroso	Dangerous
Paso prohibido	No thoroughfare
Peatones	Pedestrians
Salida	Exit

There are several signs that are not international:
Relof obligatorio is seen in some parking places in the Balearics. This means a parked vehicle must display its time of arrival. All rented cars have a plastic or metal indicator for this purpose. Note also *Ilegadas,* entry/arrival; *salida,* exit/departure.
Carga y descarga means that the space is for loading and unloading during the times indicated but at other times parking is allowed.
Transporte authorizado these spaces defined by white lines are found outside business premises such as banks and offices and are reserved for their purposes.
Vado permanente means keep clear. This is a legal sign and must be observed.

Be careful not to park where the edge of the pavement is painted red and white or blue and white.

Petrol stations

There is a great shortage of petrol stations in Ibiza and it is well to remember that they are only open weekdays from 0700 to 2100 hrs. On Sunday two are open on a rota basis. To find out which are open it is necessary to see the local newspaper, *Diario de Ibiza*. In any case, it is better to have a full tank if you intend to drive at night or on a Sunday. There are petrol filling stations located on the outskirts of San Antonio on the road to Ibiza town; at the edge of San José; likewise at San Juan; in Santa Eulalia (where there are always long queues, so be patient); on the way out of Ibiza town on the road to Santa Eulalia (this one remains open all night).

It is recommended that, if you do not speak Spanish, when you go for petrol you offer a 1,000 or 2,000 peseta note and ask for a *mille* or *dos mille pesetas gasolina;* it's easier for you and the attendant and will speed up service.

Toilets and water can be found at filling stations and sometimes there is a shop selling spares and sweets. Car wash facilities are similar to those in the UK. Petrol comes in three grades. *Extra* 98 octane, *Super* 96 octane and *Normal* 92 octane. At the time of writing *Super* petrol is 78 pesetas (£0.35) a litre. Do not confuse petrol (*gasolina*) with diesel (*gasoil*).

Petrol stations do not provide car repair services. This is a separate service called *taller mechanico*.

Self drive car hire

Car hire agencies (*aquiler de coches*) in Ibiza and Formentera include the international firm of Avis which operates from the airport. There are a number of local firms and prices can vary. A reliable way to rent a car is through your hotel reception or a travel agent. The rates usually include third party insurance; this should be noted as it is an essential requirement. In the Balearic island free mileage is included in the contract. Police patrol on motorcycles especially on main roads. There is an on-the-spot fine of 1,000 pesetas (£4.54) for failing to use seat belts. On a Sunday the roads can be busy with local family traffic.

Car rental is comparatively cheap in Ibiza and Formentera. Beware of shop window advertisements offering special discounts, as there can be hidden charges. You can be met at the airport with a car or have one delivered to your hotel, if booked in advance. Points to remember:

- Make sure that the car has passed its ITV inspection, (similar to MOT). An ITV disc should be stuck to the top right hand corner of the windscreen. This does not apply to cars registered in the current year.
- Should you be unfortunate to have an accident, follow the procedure given by the hire company found on the back of your copy of the contract. You are required to inform the company within forty-eight hours of the accident for insurance claim purposes. If no one is injured there is no need to inform the police.

Charges for car rental with Avis for a Ford Fiesta are 2,770 pesetas (£12.59 per day and 15,570 pesetas (£70.77) per week. Autos Portmany charges for a Seat 127 are 2,300 pesetas (£10.45) per day and 13,300 pesetas (£60.45) per week. There are additional charges for comprehensive insurance: for example, 600 pesetas (£2.72) daily for a Seat Panda. Petrol and a five per cent tax are not included. Prices increase with size and luxury of vehicle. International credit cards are accepted. Payments have to be made in advance and in some cases a deposit is also required, returnable when the vehicle is received back in good order. You will be required to produce your passport and International or UK driving licence. Some car hire companies are:

Ibiza Airport
— Avis Balearic Tel: 30 24 88
— Atesa Tel: 30 79 60
San Antonio
— Autos Portmany Tel: 34 06 73
Santa Eulalia
— Pitiusas Tel: 33 01 98
Ibiza Town
— Autos Ibiza Tel: 30 20 81
La Sabina (Formentera)
— Autos Ibiza Tel: 32 00 31
— Autos Pujols Tel: 32 03 25

Union Rent-A-Car in Ibiza are a popular firm with free delivery of cars to hotels and airport collection. Tel: 30 57 82/30 00 87.

Scooters, mopeds and bicycles

A scooter, moped or bicycle is a practical means of getting about to see the sights of Ibiza and Formentera. These modes of transport may be hired in most of the tourist areas at a reasonable charge. The cost of hire for scooters and mopeds includes the compulsory insurance but the hirer is responsible for any infringement of traffic regulations and fines incurred. Where necessary crash helmets are issued and must be worn. Examples of hire costs are: Vespa 200 cc, one day, 1,425 pesetas (£6.47); Bultaco 250 cc, two days 3,950 pesetas (£18); Puch Cobra, seven days 10,500 pesetas (£48); bicycles, one day, 425 pesetas (£1.93).

Taxis

Taxis have the letters SP (*servicio publico*) below their front and rear number plates, they may also have a green light showing at night and the word 'taxi'.

Taxis are to be found in all the main towns in Ibiza. In Formentera a limited number are at the port of La Sabina and the capital, San Francisco Javier. If there is no taxi rank in the vicinity of your hotel the reception will telephone for one. Telephone numbers for ordering a taxi are.
— Ibiza town (Paseo Vara de Rey) 30 16 94.
— Santa Eulalia (Plaza S'Alamera) 33 00 74.
— San Antonio (Paseo Maritima) 34 00 74,
— Formentera 32 00 52.

Taxi fares are a set price and each driver should carry a tariff which you may ask to see. There are no meters. If the driver gives you good service, such as carrying your bag, a tip will be appreciated.

Examples of fares are: Ibiza town to San Antonio 1,050 pesetas (£4.77), to the airport 700 pesetas (£3.18); Santa Eulalia to San Antonio 1,650 pesetas (£7.50), to the airport 1,500 pesetas (£6.82); San Antonio to the airport 1,500 pesetas (£6.82). They carry a maximum of four passengers.

Bus services

In Ibiza the public bus service is inexpensive though not frequent to country places but gives a good service to tourist complexes. At peak times the buses get full and it may mean standing room only. Taking a ride into the country can prove a delightful experience. It is a good way to observe the country folk without seeming too inquisitive and a friendly smile may result in some conversation.

Destinations are usually marked on the front of the bus. You must always enter from the front and buy your ticket from the driver. Remember to leave the bus from the rear. Bus stops are usually marked with the word *parada,* meaning stopping place. Bus queues are generally orderly and people line up facing the direction in which the bus is going. Buses run every day, but less frequently on public holidays. Timetables are available from the Tourist Office in Ibiza town and are published in the island magazine, *Ibiza Forecast.* The times of the buses serving your hotel or apartment are generally shown in the reception.

In Ibiza town bus departures are from three locations along the Avenida Isidoro Macabich. In front of the **Government Building;** three blocks west in front of the **Cafeteria Gran Via;** and one block further at the **Main Terminal.** Buses depart from five points along the **Calle Riquer** in the centre of Santa Eulalia. In San Antonio, buses to all places leave from the west end of the **Paseo Maritima.** There is a small bus service in Formentera; departures are from **La Sabina** and **San Francisco Javier.**

Some examples of bus services follow.

Ibiza town to San Antonio Departs every half hour from 0730 to 2200, then 2230 and 2330. Sunday departures begin at 0800 hrs.

San Antonio to Ibiza town Departs every half hour from 0700 to 2300 then 2400 hrs. Sunday departures begin at 0730, then every half hour until 2130, then 2300 and 2400 hrs.

Ibiza to Santa Eulalia Departs at 0820, 0945, 1030, 1130, 1230, 1300, 1530, 1600, 1700, 1800, 1900, 1815 and 2030 hrs. Less frequent on Saturday and Sunday.

Santa Eulalia to Ibiza town Departs at 0750, 0915, 1100, 1200, 1500, 1530, 1630, 1730, 1815, 1845 and 2000 hrs. Less frequent on Saturday and Sunday.

Santa Eulalia to San Antonio Departs 0930, 1100, 1530 and 1800 hrs; Sunday 0930 and 1100 hrs.

San Antonio to Santa Eulalia Departs 1015, 1145, 1615 and 1845 hrs; Sunday 1015 and 1145 hrs.

Ibiza town to San Miguel Departs 1300 and 1930 hrs; Sunday at 1030 and 2000 hrs.

San Miguel to Ibiza town Departs 0800 and 1530 hrs; Sunday a 0900 and 1800 hrs.

There are also frequent services from Ibiza town to the beaches of Playa D'en Bossa, Salinas Beach, Cala Llonga, Portinatx and Ses Figueras; from Santa Eulalia to Cala Llonga and Playa Es Cana; from San Antonio to Port des Torrent, Cala Gracio, Cala Conta, Cala Bassa and Cala Tarida.

Ferry boats

Unique to Ibiza are the large number of ferries that ply from shore to shore around the island. Once it was the only means of travelling from one village to another. Nowadays these boats still have a lot of trade conveying tourists from one beauty spot to another. This makes a welcome change from travelling by car or bus; often ferries are quicker and less expensive. What would be nicer than to see the land from the sea on a calm day with a cool breeze — but remember your hat and some cover for a tender skin; the sun is deceptively hot, especially when reflected off the water.

At Bahia San Antonio ferries sail across the bay all day and well into the evening. Ibiza town, Santa Eulalia and Es Cana are other places where there are regular ferry services. For example: Santa Eulalia to Ibiza town, four ferries a day, 250 pesetas (£1.14) return fare.

The car ferry about to sail from La Sabina to Ibiza. A pleasant voyage in calm weather.

Coach excursions

There is no doubt that if your holiday in Ibiza and Formentera is for a limited period, the easiest way of enjoying the sights of the islands is to join a coach excursion. These outings are well advertised in travel agents (*viajes*), hotel information folders and local newspapers. Half-, whole-day and evening trips can be booked in advance.

You may wish to make sure that your coach has an English-speaking guide and whether the cost includes a meal. Remember to take sunglasses and a hat, camera and cardigan, possibly flat shoes and a towel if a beach visit is to be included. Your tour is sure to stop at a souvenir shop, so some extra pesetas may be required. It is normal practice to tip the coach driver about 100 pesetas (£0.45).

Amongst the excursions offered is a full day **Island Tour of Ibiza.** On this you will be taken to a ceramics factory to watch one of Ibiza's famous potters at work, using his foot to turn the wheel that spins the table on which he forms the pot. After this the tour visits salt pans and a *bodega,* where the tasting of Ibiza's liqueurs is free. You may also have your photograph taken beside a camel. The coach then continues to San José, to see the marvellous village church and there you can do some souvenir shopping. San Antonio is the next stopping place with free time to explore the town. Afterwards there is a beautiful drive right across the west coast to Portinatx in the extreme north, for a late lunch and a swim.

Returning to the coach at about 1530 hrs, you then wind around the pine clad mountains and down fertile valleys, full of orange and lemon groves while one of the official guides gives lots of interesting facts and tales about Ibiza. A stop is made at an old farmhouse in the country, now a restaurant with pleasant gardens, where in the warm sunshine you sit and watch a colourful display of Ibizan folk dancing. One more stop is made at the end of the tour so that you can see and, if you wish, purchase the famous Majorcan pearls. So back to your hotel or apartment after a very full day.

If you tour **Formentera** from Ibiza you have an hour long sea trip from Ibiza harbour, with a super view of the old city, passing several small islands. On reaching the port of La Sabina, you board the coach for the drive to the island capital, San Francisco Javier, and later a stop at the Mirador Es Caló, from where you are able to see both sides of the island, from coast to coast, with the white sands and translucent blue seas making a truly memorable picture. Most of the day is spent on the beach at Es Pujol, but a visit to Xeroni caves is included. Your return to Ibiza full of fresh air and sunshine (but watch that you do not get sunburnt in the salty sea breezes on the ferry).

Other excursions include a walk round **Dalt Vila,** the old city; a **Beach Party;** a **Donkey Ride;** a **Barbecue;** visits to night clubs and the Casino. Prices vary depending on from where the coach starts; tickets can be obtained from travel agents and hotel couriers. In most cases children under ten half price and babies free.

FIVE

A-Z information for visitors

British Consul

The British Vice Consul, Mr G. Lankford, has an office at Avenida Isidoro Macabich 45, Ibiza town. Tel: 30 18 18 (24 hours).

Churches

Most Ibicencos are Roman Catholics, so there are churches of that religion in every village and town. Many of the buildings are fine and historic, especially the Cathedral of Santa Maria. In summer, notices of times of Masses in foreign languages are posted outside the churches and in some hotels.

Protestant and Ecumenical services with Holy Communion, to which all denominations are cordially invited, are given by the Reverend Joseph Yates-Round, Ibiza's resident Anglican Chaplain. They take place the first Tuesday of the month in San Antonio, the third Tuesday in Santa Eulalia, both at 1100 hrs. There is no Jewish congregation in Ibiza or Formentera.

Communications

General information on all the following communication services can be had by dialling 222 003.

Post
Post offices (*correos*) similar to those in the UK are in all towns and most villages and are generally open from 0900 to 1400 hrs, 0900 to 1300 hrs on Saturday, closed on Sunday and public holidays.

You may have letters and parcels sent to a local post office for you to collect. They should be addressed to you, surname first then initials, at *Lista de Correos,* in the appropriate town or village (e.g. Bloggs, J., Lista de Correos, Santa Eulalia, Ibiza, Spain). There is no charge for this service. When you collect your mail from the post office you will be required to show your passport as identification.

At the time of writing, postage to the UK for a letter costs 45 pesetas (£0.20) and for a postcard the same. All mail goes by air; parcels and packets can be registered and letters recorded. In shops where you purchase postcards, stamps (*sellos*) are usually sold. Tobacconists, (*estancos*) also sell stamps.

Post boxes are painted yellow, and are similar in shape to those in the UK. The exception is at main post offices, where letters are posted in boxes in the wall of the building; sometimes these are marked *extranjero* (for destinations abroad) and *insular* or *España* (for destinations within Spain). Small yellow boxes, square in shape, may be attached to houses in remote country villages.

In Ibiza town, the main post office is just off Bartolomé Roselló, round the corner from the Government Delegation Office in Calle de Madrid (look for the word *correos*). It is open week days from 0900 to 1330 and 1500 to 2000 hrs. Tel: 30 10 97.

In Formentera the main post office is in the capital, San Francisco Javier. Tel: 32 02 43.

Telephones

Telephoning from Ibiza or Formentera to the UK or other countries is simple, provided the coin box is not too full to accept further coins. This happens quite frequently in busy tourist resorts. Look for a public telephone marked *internacional;* those marked *urbano* are for local calls only. You can use 50, 25 or 5 pesetas coins; directions for use are displayed in several languages in the telphone booth. Recently some boxes have been adjusted to take 100 peseta coins. In hotels the switchboard operator will dial your number and call you as soon as you are through. Some hotels have telephones in the bedroom, a small charge is made for this service. In addition some bars and restaurants have public telephones.

When using the public telephone, first dial **07** for international calls. Wait for a continuous high pitched sound, then dial the code of the country required (for the UK this is **44**) followed by the subscriber's code and number. In cases where the code starts with 0, this is omitted. For example, for London (01), just dial 1.

International country codes from the Balearics are, Austria 43, Denmark 45, Germany 49, Holland 31, Italy 39, Portugal 351,

Sweden 46 and the UK 44. Cost indication: to the UK between 0800 and 2200 hrs, 136.5 pesetas (£0.67) per minute; between 2200 and 0800 hrs, 90.5 pesetas (£0.44) per minute. It is possible to reverse the call charge by dialling an operator on 9398, then asking for *cobra revertido*.

Telegraph

Cable messages can be passed day or night by way of the main telephone exchange. Dial 222000, 222001 or 222002.

Telex

For teleprinter service, dial 222005. For emergency remittance of money, your own bank at home can do this by telex to a Spanish bank. This service can be granted very quickly. If necessary ask permission to use a travel agent's telex number.

Currency and banks

Ibiza and Formentera are part of Spain and therefore the currency is the peseta. The coins in use are 1, 5, 10, 25, 50, 100 and 200 pesetas. Notes are: 100, 200, 500, 1000, 2000 and 5000 pesetas. The 'high street' banks are the same as in Spain and have names like, *Banco de Bilbao, Banco March, Banco Credito Balear* and **Banco de Santander.** Opening hours do vary slightly but generally they are 0930 to 1400 hrs daily, closing at 1300 on Saturdays, and closed on Sundays and public holidays. Most banks accept Eurocheques supported by the Eurocheque Card, Visa or equivalent, if displaying the appropriate sign. Be sure to check with your bank that your cheques and card are valid for use throughout Spain.

When you go to the bank you will need to take your cheques, cheque card, credit card or travellers cheques and your passport. They will probably want to know where you are staying. You can also cash travellers cheques and exchange money in travel agents and hotels. Some restaurants and shops accept Visa and Access as a means of payment. The currency exchange rate is displayed in most banks and travel agents. A small charge is made for transactions.

The larger hotels will have deposit boxes for hire for guests to lock up their valuables. The Ibicencos are generally law abiding but in busy plazas, markets and at fiesta time it is sensible to take precautions against pickpockets.

Travel agents and other businesses will change foreign currency and travellers cheques into pesetas. Look for the sign *cambio* which means change.

Electricity

Electric current voltage is 125 and 220 AC; plugs are round with two pins. Light bulbs are the Edison screw variety.

Fire precautions

Fire precautions are observed in Ibiza and Formentera, with public buildings being inspected for adequate fire escape equipment. Details of emergency exits are shown in each hotel room. Modern fire-fighting equipment is located in Ibiza town (Tel: 30 11 01).

Hairdressing

Men's barbers are called *barberia,* and ladies' salons *peluqueria.* Some of the large hotels have their own salons with prices varying according to the class of the establishment. The average price of a shampoo and set in a town shop is 800 pesetas (£3.63); a blow wave, 1,000 pesetas (£4.54); and a perm 3,000 pesetas (£13.64); a man's haircut 500 to 700 pesetas (£2.27 to £3.18).

Health

There are no dangerous animals or poisonous reptiles in Ibiza or Formentera; nor are there many flies, while mosquitos are a nuisance only when there has been rain, which is rare. The Mediterranean climate is generally a healthy one; sea breezes are to be found on most days, even during the summer months. In winter it is never extremely cold, except when the cold Tramontana wind blows from the north. Usually the greatest health problem to visitors is caused by over indulgence of food and drink, coupled with sitting too long in the hot sunshine.

Care must be taken to ensure that salad and fruit is quite clean before being consumed. *Agua potable* is water fit for drinking and *agua non potable* is not. It is suggested that if your stay is of short duration you buy bottled water (*agua mineral*) to drink. Available in supermarkets it is cheap and pleasant; it is either aerated (*agua con gas*) or still (*agua sin gas*).

Cases of upset tummies or diarrhoea are not to be expected, but should these occur avoid alcoholic drinks and salads. Take a suitable medication such as Salvacolina, a Spanish product that is available from chemists (*farmacia*). Avoid too much exposure of the body to the sun; especially it is dangerous to fall asleep whilst sunbathing. The wearing of sunglasses, hats and the early use of a suntan lotion or cream is sensible. Do not wait until the skin is turning red for that may be too late. For the first few days sun bathe only from 0900 to 1100 hrs and 1700 onwards when the sun is not so strong. (See also Medical services.)

Laundry

If you wish to have clothes cleaned or laundered, it is probably best to use the services of your hotel or apartment. It generally takes about three or four days. Maids collect laundry and a list of charges is usually put in each room. There are few self-service launderettes (*lavanderia*). Make sure that you get the correct service you require; dry cleaning is *tintoreria*.

You will be delighted with the quick speed of the drying of hand-washed clothes, even if they are not put out in the sun but left to drip in the bathroom. Washing powders and detergents are available in shops.

Medical services

Our personal experience with doctors, dentists and opticians is of a kindly and qualified service, given with every consideration being made for the fact that we were tourists in a foreign land.

A guide to medical services, with names, addresses and telephone numbers is published in the daily Spanish newspaper *Diario de Ibiza*.

Doctors and hospitals

Doctors (*medicos*) have clinics which are run in a business-like manner. In tourist resorts there would be an English-speaking receptionist. You usually get immediate attention and pay about 2,000 pesetas (£9) for a consultation; you will be given a receipt for insurance purposes. It is advisable to keep some pesetas available in case you should need emergency treatment at a time when the banks are not open, as payment is required when treatment is given. If you are given a prescription you take it to a chemist (*farmacia*) whose sign is a Green Maltese Cross. Unlike in the UK, chemists sell only medications and baby foods (not toilet requirements) but they are able to give advice and first aid.

There are also first aid posts (*casa de socorro*) which are a national service. These posts are seen in the country and buildings are marked with a red cross.

Most hotels will have the telephone number of the nearest English-speaking doctor. Numbers to ring for emergency services are:

Centro Medico Salus Ibiza An emergency medical service operating 24 hours, with a fleet of radio-controlled ambulances. The medical centres are equipped with X-ray and ECG equipment. Some staff speak English. There are centres at:
— San Antonio (Edificio Tanit, Calle del Mar) Tel: 34 00 00 & 34 11 34.
— Ibiza town (Calle Galacia 34) Tel: 30 52 57.
— Santa Eulalia (Calle del Mar) Tel: 33 08 27.
Emergency doctor service (Ibiza town) Tel: 31 16 71.
Doctor Alfredo Roig Fernandez An English-speaking doctor (Paseo Vara de Rey 16, Ibiza town) Tel: 30 12 56.
Doctor J.M. Picarzo (Avenida Dr Fleming 4, Edificio Solymar, San Antonio) Tel: 34 15 08.
Red Cross ambulance Tel: 30 12 14 (Ibiza town).
Social Security Hospital (Nuestra Señora de la Paz, Ibiza town) Tel: 30 02 00.
Hospital Insular (Ibiza town) Tel: 30 00 39.
Hospital Can Misses (Ibiza — on edge of town) Tel: 31 12 12.
Formentera medical service Tel: 32 03 56.

Dentists

Dentists (*dentista*) are fully qualified and their service is good; they use modern equipment. There are private practices and clinics (*clinicas*) where group work is done. Generally, as a tourist, you can call at a surgery and take your turn. Not many dentists will speak English, but in tourist areas the receptionist will be used to dealing with holidaymakers. Make sure that your holiday insurance covers emergency dental treatment. As with doctors, treatment has to be paid for when received. There is a Dental Clinic at Calle Canarias 10, Ibiza town. Tel: 30 19 09. Open 1700 to 2000 hrs.

Opticians

Opticians (*opticas*) provide a good service. In towns and tourist centres they are able to test your vision, without charge, and supply spectacles in about forty-eight hours. Generally, charges are lower than in the UK, with a very good choice of frames. One optician providing this service is Centro Optico at Avenida Isidoro Macabich 36, Ibiza town, and Centro Optica, Edifico Tanit, Calle Balanzat 3, San Antonio. This establishment is equipped with the latest eye-testing apparatus. It offers same day service for new spectacles and two-hour repairs. A wide choice of frames, lenses, contacts and sunglasses is available. Remember to keep your receipt if an insurance claim is to be made.

Newspapers and magazines

English daily and Sunday papers can be obtained in Ibiza town, at the airport, and in other towns where tourists stay, generally a day or two after publication. The cost is usually double the UK price. Some English and American periodicals are available and there is a selection of paperbacks to choose from if you are prepared to pay the higher prices.

There is one English language publication called *Ibiza Now* that costs 75 pesetas (£0.34), published fortnightly. It is worthwhile seeking out as it is very topical, covering a wide range of subjects relating to Ibiza and Formentera, and it includes practical information such as bus timetables and restaurants.

The local Spanish newspaper, *Diario de Ibiza,* costs 60 pesetas (£0.27).

Police

There are several types of police in Ibiza and Formentera, just as in Spain.

— The **Guardia Civil** wear a green uniform with a shiny black hat (this is now being replaced with a soft peaked cap). They are armed law enforcement officers. It is advised not to get involved in a misunderstanding with them: they rarely admit to speaking English and have a great deal of power. The Spanish authorities are determined that unruly elements will be dealt with firmly and not permitted to harm the tourist industry. Penalties are usually more severe in Spain than in the UK for similar offences. Heavy fines are imposed on those causing late night disturbances and noise.

— The **National Guard** wear a brown uniform with a beret and they are an anti-crime force.

— The **Municipal Police** wear a blue uniform; their duties are local and general.
— The **Traffic Police,** besides controlling traffic, give assistance with breakdowns and accidents. Their patrol cars are marked *tráfico Policio;* they are also to be seen on motorcycles.

All types of police are approachable and helpful, especially the Traffic Police. Some useful addresses and telephone numbers are: Guardia Civil Headquarters, Ibiza town (Can Cifre — Airport road), tel: 30 11 95; Municipal Police, Ibiza town (Calle Madrid), tel: 30 11 95; Guardia Civil, San Antonio (Calle San Vicente 12), tel: 34 05 02; Guardia Civil, Santa Eulalia (Town Hall, Plaza de la Constitucion 1), tel: 33 02 27; Guardia Civil, San Francisco Javier, Formentera, tel: 32 00 22.

Problems and complaints

Complaints about accommodation should be made on official complaint forms (*hojas de reclamaciones*); tourist offices should have these. But usually the hotel receptionist or public relations person will sort out any problem you may have; they mostly speak English.

In an extreme case it may be necessary to go to the municipal police (*policia municipal*), who are generally found in the Town Hall, (*ayuntamiento*).

Public conveniences

Public conveniences as known in the UK are seldom seen in Ibiza or Formentera but can be found in market places (*mercados*) and petrol filling stations. Look for signs marked *aseos* or *servicios,* and then *señoras* (ladies) or *caballeros* (gentlemen) respectively. Pictographs are often used; sometimes it can be a fan or a boot so some imagination is required! Generally the public use the facilities in a bar, café, restaurant or hotel. It is not necessary to be a customer though this is preferred.

Radio

A programme of music, world news, British news, sport and local information in English is broadcast every evening from 2015 to 2100 hrs. It is called Radio Popular, FM89.1 Mhz. If you wish to request

Typical of the many shops in Ibiza town, where locally made shopping baskets are a useful souvenir of your holiday.

a record, telephone 31 25 45 and ask for Brian Newman. With a short wave radio you should be able to receive the BBC World Service; programmes include hourly news broadcasts, plays, quiz games and music. It may be possible to hear BBC Radio 4 on long wave using an extension to your aerial when atmospheric conditions allow. A programme of music in Spanish is broadcast on FM 102.6 and in English between 1800 and 1900 hrs.

Shopping

Shopping in Ibiza and Formentera is very much the same as in the UK and Europe; however shops are open weekdays from 0900 to 1300 and 1600 to 1900 hrs; on Saturday they close at 1300 hrs. Generally they are closed on Sundays and public holidays. Plenty of supermarkets are to be found in the towns, and there are some in the villages. Prices are marked on most goods; remember that the metric system is used so weight is by kilogramme (2.2 lb) or part thereof. (See Appendix B for conversion tables.)

Shopping baskets and trolleys are available in some of the larger stores; any personal bags may have to be deposited at the entrance and a numbered tag given as a receipt. In tourist areas, shop assistants will understand English and generally are pleasant and helpful. In some shops you are expected to select your own vegetables, in others an assistant will serve you. At the delicatessen, meat, fish and cheese counter you will be served. It may be necessary to take a numbered ticket to get your place in the queue for service. A selection of frozen food is generally available. look for the word *comestibles* for food shops and *tiendas* for groceries.

Markets
Although grocery shops and supermarkets carry a stock of fresh fruit and vegetables, it is economical and an interesting experience to visit the local market, where fresh produce is delivered and sold daily.

In **Ibiza town** there is an undercover market (*mercado*) located a short walk from the bus terminal, along Ave. Isidoro Macabich, on Calle Extramadura. Just look which way people are coming with loaded shopping baskets! This big market, always busy and colourful, has fresh fish, meat and lots of nice vegetables.

A smaller market is in the heart of the town, just below the old city walls, near the entrance gates, in the Sa Peña fishermen's quarter. This is a *mercado payes,* the old farmers' market. Enjoy the friendly atmosphere and fresh produce like eggs straight from the farm, homemade goat's milk cheese, tender green beans and bunches of locally grown flowers. Across from these open air stalls is an undercover fish market, where you will see a variety of Mediterranean species for sale.

If you get up early in the morning there is another *mercado payes* Monday to Saturday along the Avenida Ignacio next to the Banco Urquijo Union: ten stalls are set up selling country produce. In the summer the tomatoes and melons are sweet and very reasonably priced.

There is also a vegetable market in **San Antonio.** From the Maritimo walk up the hill along the Calle Santa Innes and it is near the post office. **San Miguel,** in the north of Ibiza, has a weekly artisan market on Thursday from 1000 hrs until dusk in the main square, which is appropriately named Plaza de Mercado.

Buying clothes locally
The tourist resorts have a reasonable selection of clothes shops, including boutiques which stock modern styles. Prices range widely, bargain counters with sales goods are marked *rebaja*. It is useful to check your continental metric size before going shopping as not all the assistants will understand the English sizes. When buying in markets check that the goods are not shop soiled or flawed. Children's and baby clothes are often very attractive and colourful. Beach, sportswear, lightweight shoes and sunhats can be purchased in the larger supermarkets. There are no large clothes stores in Ibiza or Formentera.

Ibiza town is well known for its ad lib designs and smart boutiques. The 'Ibiza Look' is very suited to today's trendy casual styles. Island-made clothes are now exported to Europe and America where they are sold in high fashion salons. Even if you are not of an age group to wear such way-out gear, it is fun to window-shop down the narrow lanes in the Sa Pena district. More familiar to UK visitors is a branch of Benettons.

Souvenirs

There are plenty of Spanish made souvenirs to buy in Ibiza and Formentera, and for the holiday maker who has not visited the Spanish mainland the choice is wide. Amongst the more well known items are the exquisite **Lladro porcelain** figures and animals. These delicate collectors' pieces have price tags that start at about £10 and rise to many thousands; make sure that the piece you buy is stamped

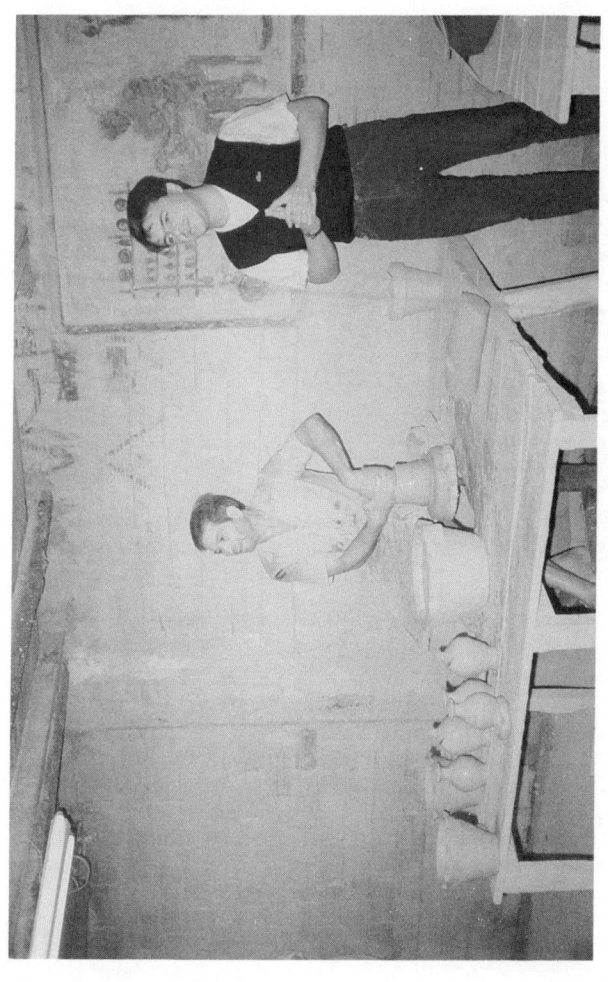

Tony the potter enjoys demonstrating his craft to tourists, with some translation by the courier, Sebastian.

with the maker's name. A cheaper version of this porcelain, made by the same firm, is called **Nao**. You will find shops in Ibiza town, San Antonio, Santa Eulalia and other tourist places which sell both products.

Beautiful Spanish **fans, costume dolls** and colourful **pottery** are displayed in most souvenir shops. **Leather items** like belts, handbags, suitcases and jackets are ready to be bought, but it is sensible to examine the quality of the stitching before purchase, and remember to keep your receipt in case you need to return any faulty goods. In some of the larger shops visitors from abroad can obtain a ten per cent discount on purchases over £50.

Spanish alcohol and liqueurs are reasonable, cigars and cigarettes cheaper than in the UK. It pays to shop around and compare prices if you can spare the time. Olives, olive oil, almonds, cheese and cakes can be taken home. Fresh flowers too, such as sweetly perfumed carnations, will last well. Tight rose buds do not keep so long but are a delight to receive as a present.

Ibiza town is a shopper's paradise with locally made ad lib **fashions,** traditional *alpargatas* — shoes made from straw and hemp — **straw bags** and baskets (but watch that you are not buying a cheap import from China). Local **pottery** is attractive, the terra cotta bowls, dishes and glazed figures are fragile but authentic souvenirs. Hand knitted and crochet garments are not cheap but wear well, especially the very thick jumpers and cardigans made of sheep's wool from Formentera. Plenty of colourful local costume dolls are to be found.

Other popular and easy to pack souvenirs are the bottles of local spirits and **liqueurs.** Flavoured with wild herbs from the islands, they are called *hierbas* and come in various sizes of unusually shaped ornamental bottles. You may wish to visit the Perlas Orquidea factory shop, on the main Ibiza to Santa Eulalia road; this gives an opportunity to see a large selection of these **man-made pearls,** always an acceptable gift. They have a ten-year guarantee. Also out of town is the so-called Hippy Market at Punta Arabi, between Es Cana and San Carlos. There, hand-made **jewellery,** clothes and *objets d'art* can make unusual souvenirs; the tiny hand-made leather baby shoes are rather appealing.

Beautiful Ibizan hand-made **lace** and crochet table-cloths, mats and clothes, although expensive souvenirs, are good value and long lasting. Look for such things in San José and Santa Eulalia.

Television

Television programmes in Ibiza and Formentera are relayed from mainland Spain. Most hotels and bars have colour TV. British TV sets are not suitable for use in Spain, including Ibiza and Formentera. TV sets may be hired from TV shops and some apartments.

Video
Video cassettes are now very popular in Spain, Ibiza and Formentera. Libraries and clubs where cassettes can be hired can be found in Ibiza town, San Antonio and Santa Eulalia.

Time

Time in Ibiza and Formentera is the same as in mainland Spain — that is, one hour ahead of Greenwich Mean Time. Spain also has a summer time; the dates vary slightly from British Summer Time. This means that for most of the summer Ibiza and Formentera are two hours ahead of GMT.

Tipping

A tip (*propina*) is expected as in the UK and on the continent, in bars, cafés and restaurants, even though a service charge may have been added. The Ibicencos are proud and well-mannered so do not make much of the subject.

Porters, maids and cloak room attendants should also be tipped ten or twenty-five pesetas, though porters at airports have a fixed charge per piece of baggage. Taxi drivers expect a ten per cent tip.

SIX

Food and drink

Ibiza and Formentera, like many Mediterranean holiday resorts, offer a wide choice of food and drink. With visitors coming from many lands and some staying permanently, the islands have a very large selection of restaurants with different menus and dishes. Most food prices compare favourably with the rest of Europe. Locally grown fruit and vegetables are cheaper than in the UK. Food in tourist hotels generally tends to be bland, but this is because they are catering for different nationalities and want to please everyone. Many visitors are wary of the unknown.

Food

Meat (*carne*) is plentiful and butchers' shops have a good selection, though cuts are different and joints for roasting have to be requested. The butcher will cut chops, steaks and stewing steak very thinly. When you require minced beef (*carne picada*), you first select your beef, then it will be freshly minced with no fat added. A *cuatro kilo* is just over half a pound weight, a *medio kilo* is just over one pound, and *un kilo* is two pounds two ounces.

Local pork (*cerdo*) is full of flavour and pork chops are on every menu as *chuleta de cerdo,* with *lomo de cerdo* being a prime cut off a leg of pork, surpassed only by *lechon,* which is suckling pig. Lamb (*cordero*) and mutton (*carne de carnero*) are less available and expensive. Liver (*higado*) and kidney (*riñon*) are cheaper and tasty. Rabbit (*conejo*) is much used in stews. Fresh chicken (*pollo*) is very flavoursome and often free-range corn fed birds can be bought in portions or whole. When you choose the latter you will be offered it with head and claws still attached but it will have been cleaned inside.

Fish is much in demand by the Ibicencos and sometimes the supply runs out early in the day as many restaurants make sea food a speciality. The market in Ibiza town has fresh fish every morning, prices are high and usually the queues mean a long wait. Varieties include cod (*bacalad*), hake (*merluza*), red mullet (*salmonete*), prawns (*gambas*), sole (*lenguado*), tuna (*atun*), sardines (*sardinas*), squid (*calamar*) and octopus (*pulpo*).

The majority of cheese sold in Ibiza and Formentera is imported from mainland Spain, Menorca and other European countries. However, Ibiza does produce a goat's milk white cheese (*queso blanco*) which is excellent with a glass of wine or a green salad. You can buy this in the markets and some village shops.

Milk (*leche*) is rarely fresh but the long-life variety imported from Holland. However, in village shops fresh milk can sometimes be bought. Tinned and powdered milk are also obtainable.

Eggs (*huevos*) are included in the stock of almost every food shop. As the demand is always high, they are fresh enough for one to enjoy a boiled egg for breakfast.

Bread (*pan*) is sold in supermarkets but the place to buy it really fresh is a bakers' shop (*panaderia*). The bread and rolls are usually light and crusty but not as crispy as French bread. Brown bread and sliced white bread for toast can also be bought. Cakes (*pastel*) may be bought at a *pasteleria,* which is often to be found open on a Sunday morning, similar to those on the Spanish mainland. The selection is mouth watering; especially good are the large gateaux (*tarta*) which you can buy whole or in portions to take away, or just eat from your hand. Sweets and chocolates (*confites* and *bombons*) are also bought at a *pasteleria*.

Tea (*té*) and coffee (*café*) of assorted varieties are on supermarket shelves but are expensive; if you are self-catering it could ease your purse to take both commodities with you. Plenty of tinned foods are obtainable; it is sensible to buy a Spanish variety when possible as it will cost less and is often much the same flavour. Spanish tinned beans (*habichuela*) are good.

Many delicious fruits are grown on Ibiza. Especially flavoursome are the grapes, apricots, peaches and melons. On Formentera the fig trees produce a large crop that can be eaten in many ways. Try them stewed slowly in red wine with sugar and cinnamon; they also make a nice change served with roast duck instead of orange.

This is the **Mercado Payes,** *Ibiza town. A small friendly market with fresh produce daily from the country, but these apples will have come from mainland Spain.*

Local dishes

It is quite possible to have a 'real English breakfast', even 'roast Sunday dinner' in some of the tourist spots; the signs are displayed outside cafés and restaurants. But do try some of the local specialities such as:-

Ayoli Garlic flavoured mayonnaise sauce.
Bacalao Codfish and tomato casserole.
Berengenas al Horno Stuffed aubergines, filled with grilled meat.
Caldera de Peix Fish soup with rice and slices of bread.
Coco Pastry tarts topped with vegetables and fish, pizza style, very good for snacks and picnics.
Empanada Meat and vegetable pie.
Ensaimada Typical Ibizan pastry, rather like a spiral croissant, sometimes filled with jam and cream sauce.
Escalduns Stews made from chicken and potatoes in an almond sauce.
Lomo con Seta Fried pork and mushrooms.
Sobrasada A bright red piquant sausage with paprika.
Sopas Payes A soup of mixed green vegetables, stock, oil and bread. It often has chick peas and meat added so that it is almost a complete meal.
Tumbet Aubergines, peppers, tomatoes and potatoes fried in oil.
Flaon Cheesecake made of local honey and herbs.
Sorfit Pages Lamb, chicken, pork, potatoes, garlic, onions, peppers, flavoured with cinnamon and cloves, simmered in their juices.
Guisado Rich soup with slices of fish and meat.
Greixeres and Bunuelos Special pastries baked at fiesta times.
Cuscusso Made from almonds, raisins and breadcrumbs and used to stuff the turkey at Christmas time.
Tapas Not a speciality of Ibiza and Formentera but served in all local bars. These are delicious bite size savouries which are eaten with a drink. Usually they include sea foods, meatballs, salad vegetables, fried fish and olives. The word *tapa* means lid; in the old days a portion of food was served on a tiny dish which was placed on top of the glass. Today these snacks make a light and tasty meal.
Paella This, the best known of Spanish dishes cooked in a special paella dish, comprises rice cooked with saffron to which meats, fish and vegetables are added. It is usually freshly prepared and takes about half an hour to cook. Generally the dish is prepared for two or more people.

Drinks

Locally produced drinks tend to be rather sweet and many of them are flavoured with local herbs. Frigola is based on wild thyme and is very sweet and aromatic. Palo is a local liqueur, bitter sweet, made from crushed and fermented carob seeds; it is usually laced with gin. Hierbas Ibicencos is a drink which comes sweet (*dulce*) or dry (*seco*) and, as the name suggests, it is flavoured with a number of herbs including rosemary, though aniseed is the distinctive taste that comes through. All these and more local drinks can be sampled during a visit to the **Camel Cellar** just off the Ibiza to San José road. Coach excursions touring the island usually make a stop there.

There is a pleasant Spanish liqueur on sale called Calisay, which is also made from herbs. Spanish brandy (*coñac*) is said to have a less delicate flavour than French brandy, and it is much cheaper. Soberano and Fundador are two brands which cost about 575 pesetas a litre and are 37° proof. Spanish gin, such as Larios and Rives, is 38° proof and costs about the same.

Sangria is a popular Spanish drink which is usually served in a jug for two or more people. It is a mixture of red wine, orange juice, brandy, mineral water, slices of fruit and plenty of ice. Refreshingly cool, it can be more potent than it tastes.

It is possible to buy English draught beer in some bars in tourist resorts. However, the local beer (*cerveza*) is a light, cool and refreshing drink.

Non-alcoholic drinks

Mineral waters and soft drinks, such as Coca Cola and Seven-Up, are plentiful. The latter can be helpful if you have a queasy tummy.

When asking for a cup of coffee (*un café*) you are likely to get a small cup of very strong black espresso coffee. If you require a large cup, ask for *café largo;* with milk it is *café con leche* or *café cortado* (a dash of milk). Best of all, try some coffee with some *conac* — a speciality called *café carajillo* is delicious and will make you feel happy.

Horchatas is a popular nut-flavoured milk. *Zumo* is the juice of many oranges, whisked, with ice if so required. *Lemumba* is a chocolate drink with brandy, drunk hot or cold. *Vino Pages* is Ibizan wine made from local grapes; wine from Formentera is red and dry with a fruity flavour, and it improves when served with ice.

Bars and cafés

These establishments are very much a way of life in Spain and the Balearics. They often open very early in the morning and will give a service until the last customer has gone late into the night. Open-air cafés are justifiably very popular with tourists, who can sit in the glorious sunshine enjoying some refreshment and watching life go on around them. You may sit at your table as long as you wish and it is not necessary to pay for your drinks until you leave. If you sit at the bar it is generally cheaper than when served at a table. A small tip (*propina*) is usual (see Tipping, chapter 5). Wines and spirits are served at all hours of the day and night.

It is quite in order for unaccompanied females to use bars and cafés; friends will meet for a chat over a glass of wine and some olives. The end of the afternoon is the time when Ibizan women take a cup of chocolate and nibble *churros,* delicious sweet fritters. Children, too, are seen at all hours in the bars and no one seems to resent their presence.

Cafeterias are not always self-service restaurants but are bars that serve meals like hamburgers, chicken and chips. The word *desayuno* indicates that breakfast is served. Usually it consists of coffee, rolls or toast, butter and jam. In tourist places British breakfasts are available.

Restaurants

Ibiza and Formentera have a variety of eating establishments which allow a good choice; excellent standards can be obtained in the several types of restaurant. An international cuisine gives the gourmet a splendid opportunity to enjoy dishes ranging from chateaubriand and lobster thermidor to paella and pizzas, home-made sorbets and fresh strawberries. Ibiza town, San Antonio and Santa Eulalia have a selection of colourful restaurants. Besides local Ibizan menus you will find places that specialise in Chinese, German, Swedish, Italian and vegetarian cooking. If you are on a package holiday, the courier will be able to advise you of a place to suit your taste and pocket. Local newspapers have advertisements that describe various places to dine and their menus.

One of the best ways to sample local food is to eat where the Ibicencos gather. Do not be shy to enter, the locals will be busy talking and are used to seeing tourists. Out-of-town bars sometimes have restaurants behind, so do not be put off if you cannot see where there is a table. Sometimes you will be pleasantly surprised and led to a delightful hidden garden patio. If you wish to please the restaurateur ask to go into the kitchen, then select your food from the steaming pots. This can be a delightful experience, especially in country areas where the whole family may gather to help you choose. When it comes to ordering it will be helpful to know that *al horno* means baked in the oven, *a la romana* deep fried, *parrilla* grilled, *muy hecho* well done, *regular* normal medium and *poco* rare (steak), *estofado* stew.

What to expect

Restaurants in Spain are graded into four categories, denoted by the number of forks (*tendores*) shown. The grading tends to reflect the price rather than the quality of the food, the higher the number of forks shown the more expensive it will be. All restaurants in Spain must display a tourist menu of the day (*menu del día*). This usually comprises a substantial soup, grilled steak or chop, salad, potatoes, bread, icecream, fruit or caramel custard (*flan*) and wine. Average price at a small restaurant would be 500 pesetas (£2.27). A number of restaurants accept credit cards.

Restaurants are open for lunch from 1300 to 1500 hrs. Dinner is normally served from 2000 hrs, but in tourist places it could be earlier. If you wish to keep the cost down, then order the house wine (*vino de casa*), it will be drinkable and half the price of the bottled wine.

A selection of restaurants
Ibiza Town

● **El Corsario** (2 forks) Pontiente 5, Dalt Vila, Ibiza town. Tel: 30 12 48. High above the port along cobbled streets, this restaurant has an extensive menu, serving simple and gourmet meals at lunch and dinner. Drinks and snacks on the top terrace, either in the sunshine or at night are instantly relaxing. Closed Sunday lunchtime.

● **Restaurant El Portalon** (4 forks) Plaza de los Desamparados 1, Dalt Vila, Ibiza town. Tel: 30 08 52. This seventeenth-century Moorish house, with valuable antiques, has two spacious dining rooms and a vine covered terrace outside, which is candle-lit at night. It is luxurious, romantic, and expensive. The multi-lingual staff are quietly attentive.

● **Cellar Balear** (3 forks) Ignacio Wallis 18, Ibiza town. Tel: 30 10 31. An old wine store now converted into two spacious air-conditioned dining rooms, this is a good place to have local Ibizan and Spanish dishes, such as *zarzuela* (a fish stew), *lechon* (roast suckling pig) and paella. Bar opens at 0900 hrs. Closed Sundays.

Dona Margarita's Restaurant in Santa Eulalia, one of the first class eating places to be found in Ibiza.

- **Alfredo's** (2 forks) Vara de Rey, Ibiza town. Tel: 30 10 00. One of Ibiza's oldest bar restaurants, it has tables and chairs in the town square. You can have authentic local dishes, fresh fish, mixed grills, steaks; drinks and snacks are served from 1000 hrs. Prices are reasonable. A good place to sit and watch it all happening in swinging Ibiza.
- **Restaurant Formentera** (3 forks) Calle Eugenio Molino, Ibiza town. Tel: 30 00 54. Situated right by the port, this easy to find restaurant is well known for its excellent local and international menu and moderate prices. It's always busy but usually you get quick service.
- **San Telmo** (1 fork) Marino Riguer 6, Ibiza town. Tel: 31 09 22. In a small waterfront cul de sac, this small restaurant offers a tempting French cuisine, with tasty dishes like pepper steak and apple tatin. It can be very busy here.
- **La Jota** (2 forks) Galaca 2. Off Avenida España (seaside), Figueretas. This a pretty street corner bistro in a quaint position offers a very large international menu, including prawn cocktails, chinese pork, rabbit in red wine, lobster, and delicious sweets. Open lunchtime and for candle-lit dinners, with mood music.
- **Sa Joveria** (2 forks) Carretera de Ronda. Set back off the roundabout by-pass road of Ibiza town, this old low farmhouse (*finca*) is now an attractive Ibizan restaurant, very popular with the local people, especially at weekends. It's a good place to eat regional dishes. Large car park.
- **Mar I Camp** D'en Bossa. Tel: 30 00 32. This English/Spanish run bar/restaurant offers traditional English Sunday roast dinners. T-bone steaks and tasty kebabs. Breakfasts, snacks and day long meals are served in the lounge or on the terrace. At 2000 hrs the Charcoal Grill is open. There's a cheerful atmosphere with sea views, music and palm trees. Open from 0900 to 0400 hrs.

San Antonio
- **Grill San Antonio** San Antonio. Walk up from the seafront by the fountains and you will soon reach this comfortable air-conditioned restaurant, where Chef Toni can be seen in his open-plan kitchen cooking on a charcoal grill. T-bones, roast beef, fish soup, shoulder of lamb are available at good value prices. It is well used by business people. Open for lunch and dinner.
- **Mei Ling Chino** San Antonio. At the end of the Maritimo is this easily located Chinese restaurant on the first floor. Enjoy chow mein 395 pesetas (£1.80), chop suey pollo 475 pesetas (£2.15), gambas 525 pesetas (£2.38), and all the usual Chinese dishes.

Rest of Island
- **Restaurante Donna Margarita** Santa Eulalia. A beautiful restaurant at the eastern end of the promenade Paseo Maritima. Supervised by the charming Donna Margarita herself, this high quality establishment is much frequented by Ibicencos. A splendid menu includes gazpacho 300 pesetas (£1.36), avocado Mexican salade 475 (£2.15), tender grilled lamb cutlets 850 pesetas (£3.86), pepper steak 1,350 pesetas (£6.14), caramel rum flambe 350 pese6tas (£1.60), gateaux 350 pesetas (£1.60). Try the condesa, made with vanilla icecream, cake, layers of crisp bitter chocolate and cream, and served with a hot chocolate sauce — a truly delicious dessert. The wine list includes Paternina, Banda Azul 575 pesetas (£2.62), Vina de Torres 850 pesetas (£3.86), Brut de Brut Cavas Hill 1,700 pesetas (£7.73). Do treat yourself to a meal here. Open 1245 to 1530 and 1930 to 2300 hrs. Closed Monday mid-day and for the month of November.
- **El Balcon de Portinatx** Portinatx. A pleasant and clean restaurant with a terrace overlooking the picture-postcard bay. Service is efficient and friendly. Examples from the menu are green salad, walnuts and Rochefort cheese 400 pesetas (£1.82); pork chops, chips and peas 490 pesetas (£2.23); quarter chicken, croquette potatoes and salad 400 pesetas (£1.82); entrecôte 990 pesetas (£4.50); sole 900 pesetas (£4.09); ice cream tart with whisky 375 pesetas (£1.70).
- **Bar Lumbi** Es Cabells. A modest bar/restaurant set high on the cliffs overlooking the sea, and run by Senor Antonio Riera and family, this is the place to relax and quietly wait for your food to arrive, while admiring the little garden where roses, geraniums, zinnias grow and bignonia climbs the terrace walls. On the menu is sole with salad 575 pesetas (£2.61); sea bream 575 pesetas (£2.61); pork chop and salad 550 pesetas (£2.50).

Formentera
- **Sa Sequia** Formentera. This small bar restaurant is right at the edge of the sand dunes near La Salinas. It has a surprisingly interesting menu which includes pork fillet with cream 875 pesetas (£3.98); T-bone steak 1,200 pesetas (£5.45); sole 700 pesetas (£3.18); paella for two 1,450 pesetas (£6.59); and fresh fish by weight. Rioja wine 725 pesetas (£3.29); beer 80 pesetas (£0.36).

SEVEN

Leisure activities

Sports and pastimes

Because of the warm summer climate and the close proximity of the sea, holidaymakers visiting Ibiza can participate in a wide selection of outdoor sports. Ibicencos, can enjoy all forms of leisure activities and keep themselves fit. Formentera, being so small, has fewer facilities and sports are usually run by hotels.

Bicycling
This sport is popular with the locals as well as tourists. You may rent a bicycle at the larger resorts and at some hotels and apartments. The island of Formentera, because it is so flat, is particularly suitable for exploring on two wheels. Some bicycles have seats for a small child. Average price for hire per hour is 150 pesetas (£0.68) and per day 450 pesetas (£2).

Bowling
There is a Bowling Centre at Avenida Pedro Matutes Noguera, Playa D'en Bossa, with regulation bowling lanes.

Bull fighting
Ibiza's Corridas de Toros (bullring) is located a few streets northwest of the port area, directly opposite the Royal Plaza Hotel. You cannot miss seeing this modern ring which seats 4,000. Seats in the sun (*sol*) cost less than in the shade (*sombra*). If you have not attended a bullfight before, it is suggested that you choose a seat in a high row and near an aisle, in case it does not appeal to you. It is worth hiring a cushion as the seats are very hard. Details of events are posted about the towns and tickets can be had at travel agents, bars, hotels and at the bullring.

Diving
There are plenty of opportunities for diving around the coasts of Ibiza and Formentera, but the use of scuba equipment is forbidden. The shores of these islands contain much archaeological treasure and the government keeps a watch on all diving expeditions. Snorkelling with a speargun requires a licence; facemasks and equipment can be bought in shops. Thousands of squid hide amongst the rocks, so the Ibizan fishermen spend long hours at weekends with their hook (*gancho*) looking for this much sought-after catch. Deep fried squid (*calamares*) is a favourite *tappas*. There is an official diving club, Seas Sports, at San Antonio. Tel: 34 29 66.

Fishing
As well as the above mentioned squid, fish in the waters around Ibiza and Formentera include red mullet and halibut, but do not expect to catch much inshore. Boats for fishing trips can be hired from several resorts. Tackle for fishing off jetties and rocks is on sale in shops.

Football
Today, this is Spain's number one sport and in Ibiza just about every village and town has a ground where football can be played. For the visitor the Sports Centre at Playa D'en Bossa may provide somewhere to practise.

Go-karting
There is a new Go-kart Club by the airport and about five kilometres from Ibiza town. It is well signposted.

Golf
Ibiza's 9-hole golf course, Roca Llisa, which is kept well watered and green, is in a lovely position in a valley on a hill. Costs are: green fees 2,000 pesetas (£9); coaching 2,200 pesetas (£10) per hour; hire of clubs 500 pesetas (£2.27). Mini golf courses are at Santa Eulalia, Es Cana, San Antonio and at Club La Mola on Formentera.

Horse racing
In Ibiza horse racing takes place every Sunday afternoon at the Hippodrome Ibiza, near San Rafael, an American-style track for trotting races. This is a most exciting sport, very speedy and

sometimes dangerous, with thoroughbred horses pulling well-sprung trotting carts. There is a restaurant and at the bars you can enjoy drinks and *tappas*.

Hunting

This is a sport much enjoyed by the Ibicencos, who love to go into the hills to shoot rabbits, quail, pigeons and other wild birds. Ibiza is well known for its excellent hunting dogs. The season is from February to October. A permit must be obtained from the **Sociedad de Cazadores y Otra Colombofila;** details can be had from the Tourist Office in Ibiza town.

Riding

There are riding stables at Santa Gertrudis, San Antonio, Portinatz and Santa Eulalia. Charges are about 600 pesetas (£2.72) per hour. This is a lovely way to explore the beautiful countryside and green hills of inland Ibiza.

Sailing

Craft can be hired at yacht clubs and at some beaches where there are sports centres, for about 800 pesetas (£3.63) per hour. For simpler tastes there is always the ubiquitous pedal boat, for hire on many beaches. (Be careful to keep inshore and watch which way the wind is taking you, and allow time to get back to the shore.) Cost about 400 pesetas (£1.80) per hour.

Sea excursions

A number of resorts have boats that take trippers out to sea or for a cruise along the coast. Those with glass bottoms are fun because the inshore waters are very clear and there is plenty to see. From Ibiza there are regular trips to Formentera that include a stop at the deserted island of Esplamador for a swim. This sandy island can also be visited from Es Cana; the all day excursion in a Jumbo Cruiser costs 2,350 pesetas (£10.68) per person.

Squash

There are two regulation championship squash courts open to visitors at the Ahmara Therma Squash on the San José road Km 2.7. Tel: 31 01 27. Another squash court is at the Sports Centre, Playa D'En Bossa.

Swimming

The beaches around both Ibiza and Formentera provide splendid swimming for all ages, plus plenty of shallow coves ideal for toddlers and beginners. Swimming off the rocks into deep water is fun for the more experienced. At Ahmara Therma Squash, Km 2.7 San José road, Ibiza, there is a sixteen by nine metre swimming pool plus whirlpool; water temperature is 39°C (102°F). Other activities there include steam baths, massage and a solarium. The majority of hotels have swimming pools with smaller ones for children. Please do not force your child into the water. Patience and gentle persuasion work much better, and a frightened child makes everyone unhappy.

Tennis

There are tennis courts in several parts of Ibiza and at a number of hotels, plus regulation courts at Ahmara Therma Squash, Km 2.7 San José road (Tel. 31 01 27); the Sports Centre Playa D'En Bossa; and the Club Tenis, Avenida de Espana, Ibiza town. Costs are about 750 pesetas (£3.40) per hour; coaching 1,000 pesetas (£4.54). Racquets can be hired. Do not book a court for the middle of the day as the sun can be more exhausting than you expect, especially if you are out of practice. Some hotels allow floodlit tennis.

Walking

Both Ibiza and Formentera are islands that can be discovered on foot. Make sure that your footwear is suitable. Much of Formentera is flat and the ground very stony, so sturdy footwear is required. Ibiza has some marvellous walks along majestic cliffs and gentle hills, covered with pine trees, hosts of wild flowers and scented herbs; your hotel courier will be able to suggest the best routes in your area.

The sign *Coto Privado de Caza* means that the shooting and hunting rights of the land are private, but it is quite all right to walk there provided that you take care to shut the gates and cause no damage. Many picturesque villages that dot the interior reward the walker with a true insight into the way of life of the Ibizan country folk.

A walk around the Las Salinas area in Formentera provides the unusual sight of salt pans in various stages of drying out. The nearby sand dunes and sea views are exhilarating, the ozone and sunshine will fill you with well-being.

Waterskiing
This exciting sport can be enjoyed at several of the larger resorts. Hotel information boards have the details and costs. At Pinet Playa there is a water ski school. Charges are about 1,000 pesetas (£4.54) a session.

Windsurfing
Nowadays this is a most popular sport. Practically every approachable shoreline has enthusiastic participants skimming the water, their multi coloured sails spreading wings like rainbow moths. Schools of instruction hire boards for about 700 pesetas (£3.18) per hour, or by the day or week, including wet suits. Some hotels have resident instructors.

Museums and art galleries

The main museums and galleries are listed below. There are also several small art galleries and art exhibitions in Ibiza town, San Antonio and Santa Eulalia; look for details on posters and at the Tourist Office, who will also have current opening times and entrance costs to all below-mentioned places.

Museo Arqueologico Plaza Catedral, Dalt Vila, Ibiza town. At the top of the walled city are well laid out exhibits of finds from all over the islands, including Carthaginian, Roman and Arabic artefacts. Bust of Goddess Tanit. Open from 1000 to 1300 hrs.

Museo Catedral Plaza Catedral, Dalt Vila, Ibiza town. The entrance is inside the cathedral. It contains church regalia, including robes and valuable silverware. Open from 1000 to 1300 hrs.

Casa de la Curia Plaza Catedral, Dalt Vila, Ibiza town. This exhibit contains Ibizan *artesania* local craft work. Open from 1000 to 1300 hrs.

Museo Arte Contemporaneo Sala de Armas, Dalt Vila, Ibiza town. At the lower part of the old city is this exhibition of modern art by international artists. Open from 1000 to 1300 and 1600 and 1900 hrs.

Museo Arqueologico Via Romana, Puig des Molins, Ibiza town. A large well lit modern museum containing relics and treasures from the amazing neocropolis of nearby Puig des Molins. There are Carthaginian terracotta goddesses, ornate jewellery, ceramics, urns and household utensils that are most interesting. Open from 1600 to 1900 hrs.

Nightlife

During the summer months in Ibiza, when the nights are delightfully warm, many people stay up until the early hours of the morning, not all seek entertainment but just enjoy being out of doors during the night.

Of prime importance is Ibiza's smart modern **Casino de Ibiza.** Situated at the eastern end of the Paseo Maritimo and by the Yacht Club, it is open all the year round from 2100 to 0400 hrs. Tel: 30 48 50. To gain entrance to the Gaming Rooms you have to show your passport or identity card. If you wish, and for a small fee, you can be issued with an admission card covering several days for roulette, blackjack and crap. Tourists enjoy trying their luck early in the evening as the stakes then are low for many games. Later, the more serious gamblers arrive and then the excitement begins.

In the same large building is a restaurant, art gallery and a night club that has spectacular floor shows. The semi-circular auditorium is arranged in tiers to allow for a maximum audience to see the very wide stage, which can be withdrawn to allow for dancing. Usually there are two floor shows a night with top class artistes appearing; at one show, for example, you may see performances by the Spanish Ballet Company, a comic turn, a magician, and the famous Supremes singing. This is a popular evening excursion from numerous hotels, and it is known that famous people, film and TV stars, frequent the Casino and Nightclub.

Over thirty discothèques are listed in the Tourist Office leaflet and many people choose to holiday in Ibiza just for their quality and reputation. Probably the most fabulous set-up is at the **Ku Discoteque,** on the Ibiza town to San Antonio road, near San Rafael, open nightly until 0600 hrs. Here fantastic sounds and lighting effects create a joyful ambience for the young in heart all night long.

In San Antonio, the centre of Ibiza's night life, disco music throbs all night. There are competitions to find Miss Sexy, Miss Topless, Miss Disco Queen, and so on. At the **Star Disco,** racy rhythms make you want to move all night, three big bars dispense the liquor, and dark and smoochy seats are waiting for you! There is music until 0500 hrs at the **Heartbreak Hotel,** Port Des Torrent, where well-known pop groups such as The Tremeloes, Led Zeppelin and Dave Dee have appeared. Amongst other popular discos are **Extasis, Kontiki** and **Playboy 2,** all in the San Antonio area.

Should you prefer something less energetic then there are masses of music bars of all sorts, with guitar bars being the most prevalent.

One such place is **La Gamba Alegre** (The Happy Prawn), Edificio Xaloc, Carretera Port Des Torrent, San Antonio. This joint English-Spanish venture has Karen and Carlos keeping the customers happy. A variety of music from the Spanish Olé to popular sing-a-long brings their customers back again and again each year for more cheery evenings.

A number of the larger hotels have evening entertainments every night of the week, and it is not necessary to be a guest of the hotel to participate in their games, bingo and dancing. There are several night excursions that can be arranged through your courier who will have the details and cost — and you do not have to drive.

Allow for drinks to be more expensive late at night, with charges being higher in places of entertainment when they are on the seafront. Entrance prices for the normal discos vary from 200 pesetas (£0.90) to 500 pesetas (£2.27); this usually includes the first drink (often soft drinks cost the same as alcoholic ones).

There are cinemas in Ibiza town, San Antonio and Santa Eulalia. When the films have not been made in Spain, the dialogue is dubbed in Spanish. During the tourist season some films in English are shown in San Antonio and Santa Eulalia. Usually there are two performances a night, at 1900 and 2200 hrs. Admission is about 300 pesetas (£1.36).

EIGHT

The Islands and their people

A short history

Over the years many different names have been given to the islands we know today as Ibiza and Formentera. Even now they are sometimes referred to by their Greek name of *Pityussae,* meaning 'pineclad'. Other names used for Ibiza in the past have been Ibosim, Ebyos, Ebusus and Yesibah, so it is easy to see how these words have been corrupted to become today's Ibiza. And the matter is not yet settled, for even now there is a move to refer to the island by its Ibizan dialect name of *Eivissa*.

It is perhaps surprising that there have been few discoveries of the remains of neolithic or early bronze age settlements on these islands, for nearby Majorca and Menorca have produced much evidence of prehistoric civilisation. According to the historian Diodorus Siculus, the islands were first inhabited by the Carthaginians in 654 BC, principally because of their strategic position in the western Mediterranean between Spain and The Levant.

Another important factor that stimulated colonisation was the discovery of large salt flats at Las Salinas. This valuable mineral was mined for export, as well as being used to preserve the catch of Carthaginian fishermen. At the same time lead was mined farther to the south of San Carlos, a product later put to good use by the notorious Balearic slingers that were enlisted into Hannibal's armies.

The Carthaginians

The Carthaginians considered Ibiza to be a holy island, believing its clay could repel harmful substances and animals. Thus they created a huge necropolis at Puig des Moulins where they buried thousands of their dead. This 'Hill of Windmills', situated on the outskirts of the modern Ibiza town and below the old city of Dalt Vila is one of the island's most famous sights. Here archaeologists have uncovered a rich treasure-trove of Carthaginian statues, jewellery, urns, tools and coins found lying in the tombs. Such is the extent of the find that it is necessary to have two archaeological museums to house all these precious relics. Amongst the most beautiful of these discoveries are the terracotta images of the Moon Goddess Tanit. These statues commonly depict the lovely goddess with her curly hair adorned by a golden crown, a neat bow ribbon on her forehead and a simple bead necklace on her shoulders. Tanit has now been adopted as the island's symbol.

At Iilla Plana a Punic colony settled and the discovery here of shells of the sea snail *muxex* suggests that the Carthaginians collected the purplmoorse dye from these molluscs. This would have been used for the dyeing of sheep's wool for rugs and imperial robes.

The Romans

In 143 BC the Romans destroyed Carthage and the island subsequently came under Roman rule, although it was allowed to maintain many of its Carthaginian traditions. Ibizan warriors assisted in the invasion of Majorca in 123 BC, led by the Roman general Quintas Cecilius Metellus. Later Metellus was officially dubbed 'Balearicus', hence the islands' collective name of the Balearics.

Under Roman protection the islands flourished: aqueducts and new roads were built, vines and olives were planted, figs were exported. With the islands' growing prosperity came an interesting moneymaker derived from the blending of an aromatic sauce composed from fish innards and called 'garum', and which was considered a great delicacy by Roman palates. Arts and crafts from this period have been discovered, in particular some Roman coins that bear the name 'Ebusus'. Some of the houses constructed then were solidly built, and part of the city walls can still be seen in Dalt Vila.

During the fifth century AD the Balearic islands were visited periodically by Vandal raiders, culminating in 426 with the capture of Ibiza by the Vandal commander Gunderic. They in turn were invaded by Byzantine sailors, and in 535 the island fell to the Byzantine admiral Belisarius. These overlords were particularly repressive and Ibiza's inhabitants remained virtual slaves up until the ninth century when the Moors arrived to bring the Balearics under Islamic rule.

The Moors

The Moors remained in the islands for nearly five centuries, and in 1116 both Majorca and Ibiza were occupied by the Almoravide dynasty of Muslims who had travelled from Morocco and other parts of North Africa. The Moorish influence is reflected in some words and names in the Ibizan dialect, and much of Ibiza's traditional dress and folk culture dates from this period.

Spanish Rule

In 1229 the young James I of Aragon set sail to conquer Majorca and restore the Balearics to Christian and Spanish rule. The sieges lasted longer than expected and it was not until August 1235 that Ibiza was finally taken. There is a story that when the forces of the Archbishop Guillermo de Montegri attacked the fortress of Dalt Vila they met stiff resistance, but were finally victorious through the betrayal of the Muslims. The ruling sheik had stolen the wife of his brother, and in revenge the brother opened a secret rear door in the walls at the height of the battle. The place in which the Christian brigade encamped was subsequently called the Field of Treason. Canon Isidoro Macabich Y Llobet, Ibiza's great historian and archivist, considered these events to be true.

It was soon after this time that the rebuilding of the parish church of Santa Maria was commenced, which in later years grew to become the great Cathedral it is today.

Pirates

Once more the islands of Ibiza and Formentera came under the threat of attacks from pirates, this time from the Saracen corsairs. Their continual invasions stimulated the Ibicencos into forming their own pirate fleet to prevent the ransacking of their villages. To the surprise of many, in particular the Berbers themselves, these new privateers turned the tables to become the famous corsairs of Ibiza. They took to patrolling the seas of the western Mediterranean, and it is from this time that many pirate tales emanate.

One of the most villainous of foreign pirates came from Gibraltar, a Captain Miguel Novell, often called 'The Pope' and about whom the Ibizan people have a story they love to tell. The notorious pirate came in his 250 ton sailing ship called *Felicity,* which boasted a dozen cannon, to attack Ibiza port. A local naval captain called Antonio Riquer, with a small frigate a quarter of the *Felicity's* size and equipped with only eight guns, sailed out to confront him. The battle raged throughout the afternoon whilst the islanders awaited their fate, but eventually 'The Pope' was sent fleeing. There is an obelisk in Ibiza's port to honour the feats of these daring corsairs.

Around this time one of Ibiza's duties was to keep its neighbour Majorca informed when danger from the Moors threatened. In 1561 Muslim ships put into Formentera to take on water before attacking Majorca at Soller. Thanks to a warning passed on via Ibiza the raiders received heavy losses and to this day Soller celebrates this victory every May.

During the first half of the seventeenth century the islands had to struggle to fight food shortages and corruption as well as marauding pirates. Defence towers, ditches and fortress churches were built, and some such towers can still be seen near the little village of Balafi, near San Lorenzo.

In 1662 another calamity befell the island in the form of the plague. The church of Our Lady of Jesus just outside Ibiza Town was turned into a hospital for the afflicted. It is reported that many died, and by 1669 the island population had been reduced to only 9,600.

During the Napoleonic Wars the Barbary pirates continued to harass the islands, but following the battle of Waterloo and the ensuing peace the presence of European warships in the Mediterranean brought the Muslim threat finally to a close. The end of piracy led to a more peaceful way of life for islanders, and the opportunity for economic advance. In 1836 the first printing press arrived on the island, and in 1852 a steamboat mail service was established between Ibiza and Majorca. Ten years later a postal delivery service on horseback was started and soon after a lighthouse system was set up.

Civil War

At the start of the twentieth century Spain was economically weak and politically unstable. Ibiza and Formentera were remote and unknown, their inhabitants wore peasant dress and lived a simple country life. In 1931 the Spanish King Alfonso XIII went into exile following an anti-monarchist election result, and the subsequent republic was fraught with bitter struggle. Finally in 1936 General Francisco Franco, leading a large section of the army, rose in revolt against the government.

The ensuing Civil War in mainland Spain had tragic consequences for Ibiza, with families divided in their loyalties between the Republican and Nationalist causes. The island changed hands several times and there were many executions. Along the west wall of the Cathedral in Dalt Vila there is a memorial erected by the Nationalists to their followers on Ibiza who were executed by the Republicans, and the names shown there represent many well-known Ibizan families.

The end of the Spanish Civil War brought an end to hostilities but no relief to the poverty in the islands, which remained severe up until the Second World War. In this conflict Spain took a neutral position, after which there began a slow recovery of the islands' prosperity.

In the 1960s the islands were given a miraculous boost to their economy when Europeans began to seek out the pleasure and warmth of southern Spain and the Balearics. In particular the new 'hippy' culture, born in North America, found the simple lifestyle of the islands attractive. The quiet country roads, the attractive countryside and the farmhouses with their mixed produce appealed to these new-style invaders. They were tolerated by the easy-going Ibicencos, and artists, poets and sculptors came and found inspiration in the green hills, blue skies and deserted sandy beaches of Ibiza and Formentera.

With the death of General Franco in 1975 Spain once more became a monarchy when Juan Carlos, grandson of King Alfonso XIII, was enthroned. Ibiza's tourist industry continued to grow, and the construction of a new modern airport enabled planeloads of package holidaymakers to visit the island. Property developers bought up land to build hotels and high-rise apartment blocks. Film stars and other jetsetters were drawn to these sunny islands where the local people are hospitable and tolerant of even the most way-out lifestyles. In this booming paradise of sun and fun, gambling became legalised and nude sunbathing was sanctioned. Thus the Ibizan people have found a new prosperity, accepting their role as hosts to countless visitors during the hot summer months, while returning in the cooler months to the peace and quiet of the pineclad hills and homesteads of their beautiful *Pityussae*.

Ibiza and Formentera today

Today the Balearic Islands are administered by a Civil Governor, appointed by the Spanish Government, who is directly responsible to the Minister of the Interior in Madrid. Majorca is the provincial capital of all the Balearics.

With the growth of tourism both Ibiza and Formentera have prospered and their whole economy is now based on their successful tourist figures. New jobs have created a gap between the ways of life of the traditional country farmers and the people who work in the tourist industry and its subsidiaries.

Nearly half the total residential population of about 70,000 on Ibiza live in the town of Ibiza and its environs. The second largest town is Santa Eulalia del Rio; then comes San Antonio Abad, the other two municipalities being San José and San Juan Bautista. Formentera has a residential population of just over 5,000 inhabitants.

Visitors from Britain top the tourist charts, which rose from 1,086,918 in 1975 to 1,718,184 in 1984. German holidaymakers outnumber the Spanish, French, Dutch and Swiss, in that order. Ibiza has a larger percentage of tourists than its sister island Menorca. As expected, the busiest month is August.

The standard of living in the islands has improved in recent years. Many households now own a car, have a modern furnished house or apartment with TV and refrigerator. The population is well clothed and most are content.

Much use is made of the old Ibizan language, Ibizenc, which is a Catalan dialect derived from Latin but with a vocabulary influenced by Arabic. The name Ibiza is pronounced 'ee bee tha', but there is a move to rename the towns in Ibizenc which is very confusing for the first-time visitor when consulting road signs and maps. For example Ibiza becomes Eivissa, San José becomes St Josef while Santa Innes is changed to Santa Agnes — so some imagination is required! Formentera does not escape this dilemma, with the capital San Francisco Javier altered to Santa Francesc de Formentera and San Fernando becoming Santa Ferran de Ses Roques.

The Ibicencos are easy going and tolerant of other people's ways and the atmosphere is very cosmopolitan. Despite this mixture they have high standards which include personal supervision of their businesses. Although wages are not particularly high, most of those working in the tourist trade earn enough during the season to allow them to return to their homes without further employment during the winter. The state education system, with compulsory schooling between the ages of six and fourteen, has created a new middle class. Municipal flats can now be rented and nowhere on the islands does one see real poverty.

In the past Ibiza has attracted a large number of artists, movie stars and hippy communes, and some of these happenings have not

Squat, flat roofed houses are kept immaculately white by the busy Ibicenco housewife.

been to everyone's liking. Today the scene is somewhat changed. The artists and the movie stars are still about, some even have homes on these happy islands. But the hippy days are more or less over, existing now as a fringe element that disturbs no one. The Tourist Office puts much stress on the fact that law and order is under control. People are still attracted to Ibiza port, where the night scene is lively, freakish and way-out. It is also colourful and entertaining. San Antonio has more bars per square kilometre than any other Mediterranean island. Yet away from these places Ibiza is peacefully beautiful and the rest of the tourist resorts provide what the average holidaymaker expects. It is no exaggeration to say that these islands have something for everyone.

The Ibizan way of life

Although the islanders are part of the Spanish community they consider themselves apart from the mainland and are proud to be Ibicencos.

Family ties are strong, and still several generations live together under one roof. The older people are very religious and attend church regularly. The country people are quite superstitious and some say that forms of witchcraft and herbal medical potions are still used. Many old women have the traditional long plaited pigtail hanging down their back, tied at the bottom with a neat bow of ribbon. They also wear the Ibizan country dress, which consists of a voluminous black skirt, black blouse and heavy black woollen shawl fringed at the edges. When working in the fields a large straw hat is worn, often turned up at the front, the hair being kept in place by a head scarf tied at the neck and worn under the hat.

The country families live in white-washed farmhouses (*fincas*), supporting themselves by keeping a few sheep, goats and pigs and cultivating potatoes, vines, olives, almonds and locust beans (carob). They then have their wine, meat, fruit and vegetables. Crops are also grown on a commercial basis. It is a fact that some country folk never go into Ibiza town, being content with their own village life. The women are particularly hard-working and toil very long hours, both in the fields and in the home. Ibizan men allow themselves plenty of spare time, which is spent in bars, talking, smoking and playing cards. Theirs has a lot in common with the Arab way of life.

At the weekend there are good-humoured family parties, and often you will see a large gathering of happy Ibicencos sitting under the shade of olive or fig trees. The grandpa (*abuelo*) and grannie (*abuela*) sit and mind the children, while the women prepare huge dishes of paella. The men, of course, will be at the flagons or skin bags (*porrons*) of wine, probably discussing football.

The younger generation tend to take their families to the beaches. Ibizan children are keen swimmers and love to play games. In the Spanish quarters of town, they still enjoy the evening stroll (*paseo*). Shopping is a time for a good gossip, catching up on the local news is as important as the purchase. It is well to remember that their way of life is more relaxed than that of chillier northern climates. The Spanish word *mañana,* meaning tomorrow, often applies. Why hurry? Enjoy your holiday!

If you want to get to know the local people make a habit of greeting them with *buenas días* (good morning), *buenos tardes* (good afternoon), and *buenas noches* (good night), and also use *gracias* (thank you). Your effort will be appreciated.

Now that the tourist industry employs the majority of the population, the old craftsmen are gradually disappearing. Nevertheless, there are still a few artisans, like Manola the glassblower, who can be seen at work at Castell des Puig, on the Ibiza town to San Antonio road. Today artisan glass-blowing is a dying industry, being replaced by factories which produce moulded glass objects. Castell des Puig is a gallery showroom for the pieces that Manola and his two apprentices create. Bowls, vases, plates and sculptures, every piece is unique. Most of the production is shipped to the USA, but for those who are fortunate to see Manola at work and then purchase a handmade glass object, it is a rare experience.

Another dedicated craftsman who is prepared to let the public see him at work is Tony, a potter who gives a lively and amusing display of moulding clay for original ceramics. (Can Negre is not too easy to find and it may be better to visit as part of an Island Tour excursion. Should you wish to make your own way, then take the new motorway from Ibiza town towards San Antonio. At the industrial estate you will have to turn left across the traffic — there are indications to move into the middle lane. Turn into the lane by Exclusivas Santiago, where you will see a hand-painted direction to Can Negre.) Using only a foot-pedalled wheel to turn his lathe, Tony has been making pottery for over thirty years, selling direct to the public. His figures of Ibizan women are distinctive but little of the work is glazed.

Now that Spain is a member of the EEC, Ibiza and Formentera will no doubt move towards a modern way of life. We hope that they are able to retain their individual friendly character.

Music and dancing

The Ibizan people are very fond of music and dancing, which remain a special part of their celebrations, not only at fiestas, weddings and parties but also at simple family gatherings. In towns you will hear the workmen on building sites singing, likewise children at play often sing and dance with their games. Although much of the youth in the islands now indulge in the modern trend of pop music and disco, there is still a strong element of old cultures remaining.

The **Grup de Ball Pages Es Broll** is a folkloric group that has gained much popularity and taken part in many festivals with great success. For the holidaymaker who has limited time, it is suggested that a visit be made to **Finca Can Truy,** an old farmhouse now converted into a lovely restaurant and tea gardens. The place itself, English-owned, is delightful; the 300-year old building has been carefully restored and the grounds are planted with an interesting variety of shrubs and plants. Finca Can Truy is located on a left turning off the Portinatx to Ibiza town road going towards Santa Eulalia.

All this makes a pleasant rural setting to see folk dancing. During the holiday season regular performances are given on a small stage set up in the gardens. Music is played on a wooden flute and small drum and the dancers use singularly large castanets. The music, though similar to Catalonian, has a strong Moorish influence, especially in the rhythm. Most of the dances represent village life, the sowing of corn, the courtship of lovers and bridal dances. Perhaps the most notable feature of the dances is the fact that the girls are demure, even shy, and dance with downcast eyes and slow sliding steps, while the men are almost arrogantly agile, leaping about with a great display of arm movements and high kicks.

Costumes

The folk costumes are worth a special mention, for those seen at Finca Can Truy are authentic and much care has been taken to see that they are exact replicas. The embroidery and handwork are exceptionally beautiful. This friendly group pose patiently so that the visitors may take endless photographs.

The women's dresses vary considerably but all have voluminous skirts. It is said this was to make the girls look pregnant: in the old days the Moors would come and steal maids from the villages, but they were not interested in future mothers! Under the skirts are many petticoats, the number denoting the wealth of the family. The blouse is high-necked and long-sleeved; a fine silk shawl, often carefully hand embroidered and tassled, is worn over the shoulders. On the head a large mantilla or black hat, is worn and the hair is long and plaited, tied with a ribbon. The colour of the ribbon has a meaning: red indicates the girl is unattached, yellow that she is betrothed, blue that she is married, and black that she is in mourning. Incidentally, a widow is expected to wear black and mourn for twenty-five years; then she may wear brown. Round the neck the women wear a gold scapular with images of saints, and holy crosses, and all the family jewellery, which is passed down from generation to generation. Much is gold filigree, like an *emprendada,* a necklace of Moorish design. In addition, many heavy rings are worn. The shoes are usually made from woven straw and hemp (*alparagatas*); sometimes they have open toes and are secured round the ankle with one tie.

The men wear baggy white trousers, wide at the thighs and tight at the ankles, and a loose white shirt over which is worn a black corduroy or cotton jacket. They have bright red cummerbunds round the waist and coloured neckerchiefs. There hats are very distinctive, for they are bright red and similar to the Catalonian beret, worn pulled down to one side to resemble a cock's comb. The likeness is very striking during some of the dances when they leap in the air and shout 'ye ye ye' in a bragging manner — like a cock crowing. The older men sometimes wear a black felt hat with a wide brim.

Dances

The dances are easily understood. The most common one has two phases: in the *curta* the woman dances a figure of eight with slow modest steps whilst the man, playing the large castanets, leaps about her; in the *llarga* the woman dances a large circle and the man struts even more confidently, until the woman yields and the man drops on one knee making a nice ending to the dance. There are many more of these symbolic dances and songs of the Ibizan folk, all delightfully refreshing to watch. It is good to know that some of the youth of today are keeping alive the old traditions.

Folk dancing exhibitions are also given in the village of **San Miguel** in the north of Ibiza every Thursday. During these, ancient customs and folklore are explained and local wine is tasted. You can go on a coach excursion or by bus.

Fiestas and folklore

The fiestas of Ibiza and Formentera are still celebrated with fervour by the older Ibicencos and with jollity by the younger generation. These occasions are mostly based on saints' days or religious festivals.

Nowadays, with the tourist in mind, some of the displays are more like a carnival with fireworks and games. However, the sombre religious processions, often by candlelight, do take place. Visitors are welcome to take part when due respect is observed.

Remember that fiestas are public holidays and everything in the location will be closed, except the bars and restaurants. Bus services are limited and the roads become extra busy. Quite often after the religious procession there are displays of folk dancing and singing, and Ibicencos wear their traditional costumes. It is delightful to see little children dressed in identical outfits to their parents, even babies in pushchairs wear mini-costumes. Usually the happy family will allow you to take a photograph when approached politely.

The principal fiestas and festivals in Ibiza and Formentera are:

17 January	**San Antonio Abad** Patron saint's day and blessing of animals.
12 February	**Santa Eulalia del Rio** Patron saint's day.
19 March	**San José** Patron saint's day.
Holy Week	**San Miguel** Procession on Thursday. **Santa Eulalia** Procession on Friday afternoon. **Ibiza town** Procession on Friday night.
1 May	**Santa Eulalia** Fiesta and flower show (Sunday)
23, 24 June	**Ibiza** Saint John the Baptist Day: fireworks, bonfires and festivities. On 24 June, landowners and tenant farmers make verbal contracts for coming year.
16 July	**Ibiza town** Processions and regattas in honour of the Virgen Del Carmen. **San Antonio** The same events on following Sunday.
25 July	**Formentera** The most important fiesta in honour of Saint James; processions, folk dancing and singing.
4 to 8 August	**Ibiza town** The capital honours its patron saint Senora Maria de las Nieves: religious services; bands, fireworks, folk dances and sporting events.

24 August	**San Antonio** Saint Bartholmew's Day: high mass, concerts, processions, fireworks, sporting events.
8 September	**Santa Eulalia** Fiesta de Jesús: religious and popular festival.
29 September	**San Juan Bautisa** San Miguel's Day: arts and crafts.
1 November	**Ibiza and Formentera** All Saints Day: special cakes, pastries and nuts sold in markets.

Calendar of Spanish national holidays

January 1	— New Year's Day
6	— Epiphany
March 19	— San José
variable	— Good Friday
	— Easter Monday
May 1	— Labour Day
variable	— Corpus Cristi
	— Ascension
June 29	— San Pedro and San Pablo
July 18	— National Day
25	— Santiago Apostal
August 15	— The Assumption
October 12	— Día de la Hispanidad
November 1	— All Saints
December 8	— Immaculate Conception
	— Christmas Day

Island Flora

Both Ibiza and Formentera are a botanist's delight, because the range of soils and types of landscape are so varied: wooded mountains, fertile valleys and sandy coastline, provide habitats where wild plants and rare flowers thrive. These, with the abundant cultivations of almond and olive trees, citrus fruits and ground crops, create a continuous backdrop of glorious colours and sweet fragrances.

Early January sees the delicate mimosa bushes bringing a splash of soft yellow and a sweet fragrance to the air. It is closely followed in February by the pink and white almond blossom which carpets the fields with fallen petals. In March the golden gorse and the tall blue iris spread more cheer. Fields of white daisies in April tell that spring is here; buttercups and the little bee orchids (*Ophrys Apifera*), are now seen.

Tall palm trees provide shelter from the midday sun by the pool at the Hotel Palmyra. At night time the floodlit gardens are a romantic setting.

As the corn ripens so the red poppies wave in the breeze and the grasses in the hedgerows grow tall. By August the land is becoming dry, but into bloom come the beautiful white scented daffodils (*Pancratum Marimum*) along the sand dunes. Autumn arrives turning the vines from green to copper red and later tinging them with purple. In wooded areas the pink heather bushes (*Erica Arborea*) grow two or three metres tall. Along the fields the prickly pear cactus (*Opuntia*) bears its yellow fruit; beware of picking one, for they are covered in white spines that can inflict a nasty incision in the finger. So to the end of the year, when the orange and lemon trees are heavy with their fruits and pine cones are gathered to put round the Christmas trees.

Certainly one of the most abundant trees is the Aleppo pine, (*Pinus Halepenis*) seen growing from mountain tops to beside the sea, and sometimes a good indication which way the prevalent wind blows, for in open windy areas its trunk bends and grows almost parallel with the ground. Used over the years for building boats, its resin is used for making a pitch; the country folk still cut the lower branches to burn in their bread ovens. Another Balearic tree that grows only on Ibiza is the kermes oak (*Quercus Coccifera*). In ancient times the leaves were host to the scale insect *Coccus Ilicis;* the female was collected and dried, then used as a basis for a scarlet dye. The word kermes comes from the Arabic word *qirmazi,* meaning crimson or carmine.

Within Balearic woodland we find the diminutive dwarf fan palm tree *Chamaerops Humilis.* In Ibiza and Formentera it grows on coastal cliffs. The leaves of this pretty palm can be dried in the sun, then braided to make cord, which is then woven into baskets and chairs.

Yet another familiar tree on Ibiza and Formentera is the *Pitera Algave Americana,* which originated in the warm deserts of Mexico. Once of vital importance, this sturdy plant is to be found in almost every country *finca*. From a central bud, the *Pitera* extends long blue-green leaves with prickly spines; these can grow to two metres long and twenty to twenty five centimetres wide. Down the centre of each leaf is a sticky sap and fibrous substance. It is this thread that is dried and the hemp-like strands woven into the typical *alpargatas,* the sandals traditionally worn by every member of the family.

No description of the flora of these islands would be complete without mentioning the splendid variety of herbal plants. Rosemary, thyme, chicory, fennel and garlic are amongst the most well known and widely used. If you are not able to get into the countryside to pick these herbs for yourself, you can buy them in the local markets at a low price.

The reader who wishes to identify some of the many botanical species found in Ibiza and Formentera, would do well to obtain a copy of Anthony Bonner's book entitled *Plants of the Balearic Islands* (see Bibliography in Appendix D).

Garden plants

Compared with Majorca, there are few public gardens to be found in Ibiza and Formentera, although in the new *urbanizaciónes* and hotels shrubs and trees are planted. It is in the villas, private house and farmhouses that one notices a great riot of colour. In such a mild climate, sub-tropical shrubs and flowers bloom freely.

All over the islands the square white houses make an outstanding background for many rose beds and scarlet geraniums in pots and urns. Trellis and arbours are brightly laden with honeysuckle, red bougainvillea, blue morning glory and the bright orange bignonia vine. During the hot summer zinnias, dahlias, sunflowers, lilies and carnations provide colourful floral displays.

Tall ornamental palms, pampas grass, oleanders, hibiscus and tropical cactus provide contrast. Around every doorstep, whether it is a grand villa or rustic cottage, plants spread their green foliage, terraces and balconies drip with pot plants, for the Ibicencos love to grow things. Inside many a simple home, the floor and fireplace has cool ferns and pots of herbs; churches and cemeteries are adorned with loving gifts of flowers.

Wildlife

There are no harmful wild animals, venomous snakes or insects in these islands. The only vicious thing you might encounter is a mosquito after a rainy day. In the fields are mice, rats, rabbits, weasels and hedgehogs. Along the hedgerows, butterflies and dragonflies float in the breeze.

Ibiza and Formentera are in the flight path of many migratory birds; birdwatchers will enjoy classifying the different species, such as the brilliantly coloured hoopoe and the white egret. A walk in the woodlands and pine forests could reveal willow-, wood- and reed-warblers, white-throats and black-caps. Overhead one sees the red kite, golden eagles and even the rare Eleonora's falcon has been sighted. The river near Santa Eulalia and the salt pans of Las Salinas are areas where it is worthwhile taking field glasses. On Formentera, too, the Las Salinas salt lakes and surrounding sand dunes can be rewarding for the birdwatcher. A useful handbook to have is *The Birds of Britain and Europe.* (See Bibliography.)

Near to the built up areas the cooing of flocks of pigeons, and the twitter of sparrows mingle with the songs of blackbirds, finches, parakeets and yellow canaries in birdcages, hung outside the doors of Ibizan homes. On warm evenings you hear the cicada, that winged chirping insect so evocative of Mediterranean summer nights. Look out, too, for the tiny lizards with a long tail, known as geckos. Shy and harmless, they dart away almost before you see them. Do them no harm because they catch mosquitoes.

Native dogs

One of the oldest known breeds of dog is the Ibizan hound, the *podenco,* seen at Cruft's Dog Show in London. This celebrated hunting dog is very skinny, and its coat is white and pale pinkish brown. It looks like a small greyhound, with long nose and big alert ears. The eyes are pale and red rimmed. The pedigree of this dog can be traced back thousands of years and pictures on the walls of ancient Egyptian tombs show a similar type of hunting dog.

NINE

Ibiza town

Rising into the blue skies Ibiza town, the island's capital, is a sight that all visitors remember. For it has as a crown the incredible bastion of Dalt Vila, the old city, whose solid walls protect its ancient castle and Gothic cathedral. Below this massive fortification lies the fishermen's old quarter, Sa Pena, with many winding streets hugging the water line, its Moorish houses giving an air of mystery. To these have been added the modern port and tall buildings of today's busy town, full of colourful people who share with the friendly Ibicencos the pleasure of being in such a delightful place.

All who visit Ibiza should be sure to include a tour of Dalt Vila. If walking cobbled streets and steep steps is a problem, then it is worth hiring a car or, better still, a taxi to get up to the cathedral square. But if you are in good health then choose a bright cool morning for your expedition into the past history of Ibiza. The walk described takes about two hours.

Dalt Vila

Dalt Vila is one of the finest ancient preserved cities in Europe with most of its solid walls still intact. The city boasts of an impressive history; although most of the existing fortifications date back more than four hundred years, there are remnants of earlier buildings and walls built over two thousand years ago.

The Carthaginians founded the city in 654 BC, calling it Ibosim. When it was occupied by the Greeks they called it Ebysos; then came the Moors who named it Yebisah. The ramparts that we so much admire were built in the sixteenth century after the Christian reconquest of the island by Spain. Today they are declared a national monument.

Dalt Vila has three entrances but only two are in daily use: the Portal Nou, off Avenida Ignacio Wallis is for pedestrians only; the main entrance of **Portal de las Tablas,** where this tour starts, is behind the Church of San Telmo and the little market. Traffic is allowed through this entrance but there is no pavement so beware.

As you slowly walk up the slope, originally the moat, and you reach the massive **Portal de las Tablas,** pause and look at the coat of arms of Aragon and Castile. The Latin inscription tells us that the walls were completed in 1585 by King Philip II of Spain. On either side of the archway are two white headless statues; they were unearthed from this spot during the sixteenth century and, according to feint Latin inscriptions, one statue honours a Roman senator and the other is a tribute to Juno the Roman goddess.

Now you walk through a dark tunnel across cobblestones that must have been pounded by many famous warriors and statesmen of the past. You are brought back from your imaginations by a present day vendor selling trinkets and souvenirs. On either side massive walls block out the sky. A turn to your left, still climbing, reveals a small quadrangle, the **Patio de Armas** (arsenal square) where in the past troops stored and received arms. Nowadays it is alive with attractive restaurants and artisans displaying their jewellery and ceramic ornaments, but not all of it is handmade. Look for the little shop where you can buy high quality handmade leather work. Here sandals are made to measure and ready in twenty-four hours.

From this point the old city becomes a maze of narrow cobbled streets and alleyways. By government order all the houses are painted a brilliant white, an amazing sight in the strong sunlight. Many of the tall houses have small balconies with wrought iron railings, where bright geraniums and carnations mingle with lines of washing hung out to dry. Before you climb higher you may like to pause and visit the museum of modern art, **Museo Arte Contemporáneo** (small admission charge). In what was the city hall, some ninety paintings by modern artists are displayed. It seems an incongruous exhibition to have in such ancient surroundings.

Carry on the tour by climbing upwards to where all roads lead eventually, the **Plaza Catedral** (cathedral square). There are plenty of places to pause and get your breath, and glimpse through wrought iron gates, cool patios full of ferns and hanging vines or walls bright with bougainvillea and other colourful creeping plants. Old and stately houses have coats of arms, and great heavy doors between slender columns either side of the portico.

A steady climb uphill through Dalt Vila passing many fine old houses with wrought iron balconies, leads to the Cathedral.

When you find yourself at the end of **Avenida Generalissimo Franco,** which is also known as **Sa Carossa,** you will reach **Bastion Santa Lucia** and the sixteenth century **Church of San Domingo.** Next to it are the offices of the **Ayuntamiento** (city hall). Across from there enjoy fine views over the port and the sea to Formentera.

Continue along the **Calle Santa Maria.** Here you may care to admire a very lifelike statue of Isidoro Macabich Y Llobet, the Ibizan historian who died in 1973. Not much farther up and you have reached the **Bastion Santa Tecla** and more good views. These bastion walls, which number seven, took thirty years to build, having been originated by the Emperor Charles V in 1554; they are named after saints. It is a credit to the stonemasons who built these walls nearly two and half metres thick that they have remained mostly intact to this day.

The **Catedral de Santa Maria de las Nieves** (Our Lady of the Snows) was built on the site of a Roman temple and a Moorish mosque. Founded by Guillermo de Montegri in 1235 when he and other leaders of the Reconquest pledged to build a mighty church, it was renovated in the sixteenth century and again in the eighteenth, when it was created the Cathedral of Ibiza and Formentera. Today it is necessary to pay about 50 pesetas (£0.23) to enter the cathedral and a further 50 pesetas to go inside the **Sacrosant Museum** (open 1000 to 1300 hrs) which houses magnificent ecclesiastical robes, vestments and church regalia. The interior of the cathedral is usually busy with tourists; nevertheless its white austerity is impressive.

By the west wall is a memorial to the Nationalists who fell in the Spanish Civil War. It contains names from all the main Ibizan families who suffered greatly at the hands of the Republicans. Across the Plaza and down some steps, is the entrance to the **Museo Arquelogico de Dalt Vila.** Recently modernised this is a very pleasurable place to visit for all the exhibits are well lit and easily seen. Some of the great treasures of the Carthaginians are on display here, all having been discovered in the islands. Priceless urns, coins, jewellery and statues are closely guarded and no cameras are allowed. Unfortunately the written descriptions are only in Spanish. It takes about half an hour to see all the exhibits.

There is still a little farther to climb up before reaching the old castle, which is falling into disrepair and not open to the public. While there you may be glad of some refreshment before your walk down hill. A small bar will provide drinks; there is a toilet but no restaurant.

Seen in Dalt Vila, an Ibicenco craftsman sits outside in the sunshine making Alpargatas sandals.

By altering the route of your descent you can pass other delightful corners and alleys, discovering more artisan shops and boutiques. If you are fortunate you will come across one of the local shoemakers sitting in the sun, busy making authentic *alpargatas,* the Ibizan sandals woven from hemplike *Pitira Agave* thread. When you leave by **Portal Nou,** the new gate, you are back in the modern part of Ibiza town. It comes as something of a shock to be amongst noisy traffic after the peace, quiet and charm of historic Dalt Vila.

Sa Pena and La Marina

This walk around Sa Pena and La Marina takes about 1½ hours. Begin down at the harbour of Ibiza town, where there is a bare granite needle obelisk, which is one of the island's most famous landmarks. **Obelisco a los Corsarios** is believed to be the only monument in praise of privateers. In the past Ibiza and Formentera were so plagued with pirates (*corsarios*) that some of the Ibicencos decided to defend themselves and they took to sea to do just that. They in turn became very bold privateers (see Chapter 6).

Opposite the obelisk seawards are the new offices and dock terminals for passengers and vehicle ferries and cruise liners. Upstairs is a pleasant restaurant used by the locals as well as travellers.

Inland from the monument is a traffic-free road where there are restaurants and the houses of the fishermen's old quarters known as **Sa Pena.** Still occupied by many Ibizan fishermen and their families, the tall white houses remain unchanged by modern development, except for the host of TV aerials. A number of streets are closed to traffic, being only wide enough for donkey carts. Day and night the streets are thronged with tourists and the 'pretty people', who adopt the free and easy attitude of wear what you like, do as you please. Nevertheless the place is orderly; two policemen are visibly about most of the time, so the authorities have the situation in hand.

It really is a fascinating unusual place, so small you will never think that you can get lost; but you may suddenly find yourself outside the same boutique having gone round in a circle! This is a lovely spot for souvenir hunting, among lots of straw bags and baskets, hats, shoes, brown thick pottery dishes and beautiful Spanish ceramics. You'll find plenty of open-air cafés to rest your weary legs, then off you go again looking for spices, coffee and the market. If you want an expensive leather or suede jacket, perhaps

Sa Pena, old fishermens quarter, provides good shopping and colourful for tourists.

with hand bag and shoes to match, some smart pants or a way-out top, here is the place — but you will need lots and lots of pesetas.

Without noticing you have wandered into this part of town known as **La Marina,** for there is nothing that seems to separate it from the Sa Pena district, except that it runs along the port. The **Church of San Salvador** is where on a Sunday morning you are likely to see Ibizan women wearing the traditional costume. Apparently they are used to the eternal photographer, but do not get too intrusive: they are on their way to Mass and not there as a tourist attraction.

It is on the corner of Avenida Andenes and Avenida de Santa Eulalia, right by the port and La Marina that the road entrance to the docks is guarded by a policeman and there is a barrier. Only traffic about to board the ferry is allowed to enter, and then just an hour before sailing. It is here, too, that passenger and vehicle ferries depart for Formentera. Tickets can be purchased at a kiosk or from travel agents (*viajes*). Continue along Avenida de Santa Eulalia; in just a few yards is a yacht marina and the **Club Náutico Ibiza.** The tall modern apartment blocks across the road have a fine view of the harbour, the old town and castle.

Ibiza, the modern town

Although this tour is through the modern part of Ibiza town, we are starting it at the **Paséo Vara de Rey,** which lies quite close to the port entrance, by the traffic lights. Lined with shady trees and hard seats, this boulevard is the meeting place for businessmen, housewives, families and friends. At one end is a busy news-stand which has a good selection of European newspapers, magazines, picture postcards and maps. In the centre of this promenade is a dramatic statue to one of Ibiza's heroes, Joaquin Vara de Rey, hence the name of the road. This Spanish general fought in the Spanish American War of 1898 and he and five hundred Spanish soldiers died in action defending Santiago de Cuba against a much larger American force. Because of his courage the Americans buried him with full honours and the memorial here in Ibiza shows the general with sword aloft and winged angels below.

Along one side of this boulevard are open air cafés and restaurants, where it is nice to sit and watch the passing scene; there is car parking too, but you will be fortunate to find a vacant space at any time of day or night. On the other side is a taxi rank and the

Tall elegant old houses line one side of the Plaza Vara de Rey.

street is lined with small shops and offices. Here is the **Tourist Office,** thoughtfully open at 0830 hrs so that holidaymakers arriving early on the ferry will find somewhere to get information; we suggest you ask here for a town and island map and times when museums are open as this can vary. Usefully placed close by are the offices of Iberia Airways, the travel agents Viajes Melia and the Banco de Bilbao. At the western end of the road the modern blocks of the new town crowd around.

Here you turn into the **Avenida Ignacio Wallis,** going left at Avenida Isidoro Macabich if you want the bus stations. The Post Office is in Calle Madrid, a turning off Isidoro Macabich, just before the imposing building of the **Consell Insular de Ibiza y Formenter** and the **Town Hall.** To get to the main undercover market, you continue along the Isodoro Macabich and turn left into Calle Abad y Lasierra.

From the Town Hall and Plaza Enrique Farjarnes, turn south and walk along **Calle Obispo Huix,** crossing the busy Avenida de Espana into Calle de Leon. At the end of the road you turn right and across the Via Romana is the important building of **Museo Arqueologico** (yes, the same name as the one in Dalt Vila). Behind the museum is the **Puig des Molins** (Hill of Windmills), still wild and in a natural state. This is where the Carthaginians, and later the Romans, brought their dead to be buried in the clean air of Ibiza. This necropolis, which may be visited, has over four thousand tombs. Several typical burial chambers have been cleared and are illuminated. After you have had enough of this rather eerie place, do allow time to visit the museum. You will be surprised at what wonderful treasures and artefacts have been recovered from the tombs, even though they were pillaged by the Moors.

The Archaeological Museum of Ibiza was founded in 1907. Over the years it has been extended and modernised and in its present form was inaugurated in 1981. In well lit and spacious rooms on two floors are exhibits which are truly fascinating, even to the ordinary person. You will surely be awed by the beautiful terracotta head of the **Goddess Tanit,** with a gold crown and bow in her hair, and brightly coloured beads, necklaces, gold rings, bangles and amulets. Huge ostrich eggs (*huevos de avestruz*) decorated with perfectly symetrical designs, graceful urns, vases, goblets and ceramics have been carefully restored. Some of the objects may seem less beautiful, such as death masks, crude primitive and phallic figures. Unfortunately all the notations are in Spanish only, but

Seen in Ibiza town. An old country woman seeks assistance to cross the road.

there is a very useful leaflet in English, obtainable there for 50 pesetas (£0.23), which gives an interesting description of the necropolis and of some of the treasures.

Thus there is plenty to do and see in Ibiza town during the day, but it is the night time scene that attracts many visitors, when the flashy and expensive boutiques broadcast the latest music, and street bars and cafés vie with one another for your custom. The hiss of the gas lights of the street traders, children at play, wandering musicians, and eccentrically dressed extroverts strolling by oblivious, too wrapped up in their own glorification, all contribute to its singular ambience. The placid Ibicencos amongst the crowds, gossiping on the street corners or shopping for cream doughnuts, olives and garlic, accept it as a matter of course. You can smell the aroma of coffee and spices under this wonderful warm night sky, while all the time above are floodlit turrets and battlements of Dalt Vila. You will remember Ibiza town.

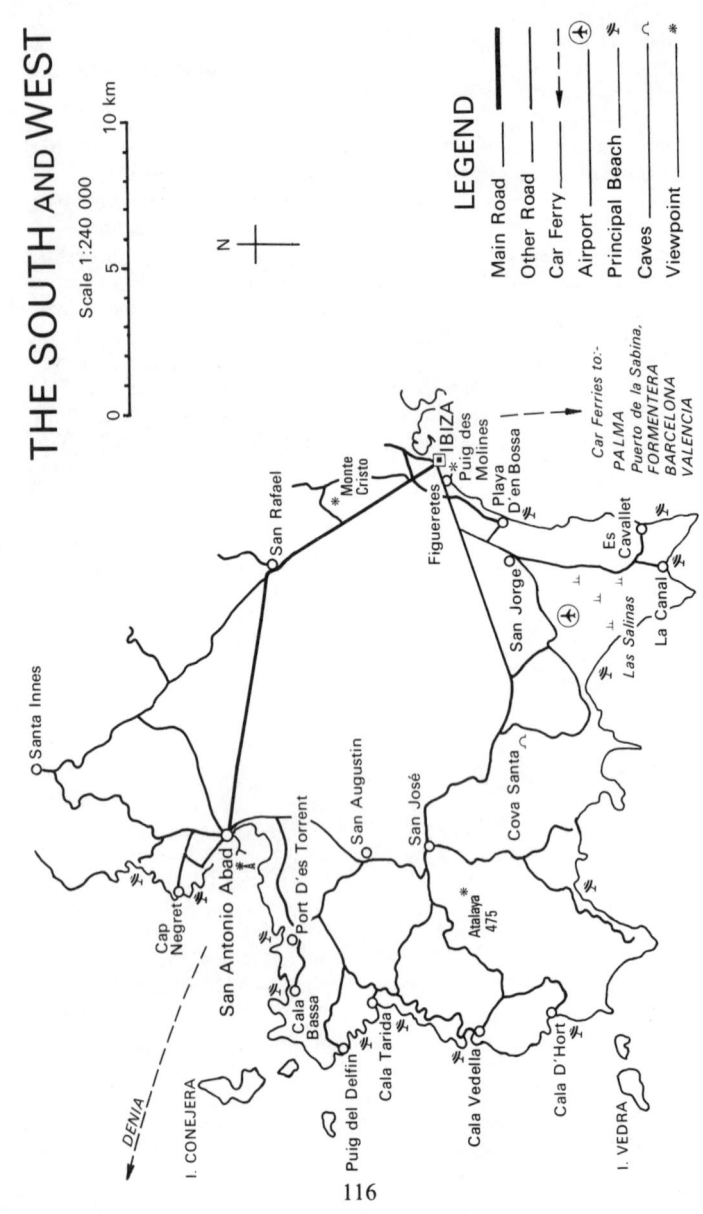

TEN

Touring Ibiza: the south and west

It takes hard driving to see all of Ibiza island in one day; two days will allow time for a quick look at the major places of interest; with three days you could see most of the beaches as well. Of course it is far better to tour at a more leisurely pace. Ibiza has lovely inland country and tucked away are quiet coves. Because of the sea crossing a full day is required when visiting Formentera.

The tour of the south and west of Ibiza described below begins and ends at Ibiza town, and takes you through Playa D'en Bossa, Las Salinas, San José, Cala Vedella, Cala Bassa, San Antonio, San Rafael. You need to allow one full day for this trip of around 133kms.

Playa D'en Bossa and Las Salinas

Our starting point is Ibiza town, but the route can be adjusted to commence at any of the resorts. Leaving town by the **Avenida de Espana,** you soon reach a major roundabout so look for route signs and keep to the correct lane as you travel the roundabout: your direction is marked Puig Molins, Figueretes, Playa D'en Bossa, almost a full circle. At first you may think that you are not on a major road, the surface is full of pot holes (unless they have been repaired) and in places there are no proper side pavements. This is **Figueretes,** full of rather tall ugly modern apartments and an assortment of small shops, bars and restaurants. Behind, on the Puig des Molins, is where the great Carthaginian necropolis was unearthed.

To reach Playa D'en Bossa, you continue going westwards passing several large tourist hotels en route. Here small side roads lead to the sea. A new holiday resort, **Playa D'en Bossa** is still being developed and enlarged, right along the seven kilometres of magnificent golden sands washed by the warm seas. Here are straw sun umbrellas, pedalos, wind-surfing, water ski, sports centres, mini-golf, riding and everything one needs for a beach holiday, including night life in the hotels, discos and nearby Figueretes. This is a holidaymakers' playground only ten minutes drive from the airport. Buses run regularly to Ibiza town.

By taking the road marked 'Airport' and 'Go Karting' you now join the busy main airport road which passes through the old village of **San Jorge.** You may wish to stop to visit its fourteenth-century church, one of the oldest on the island. It is very unusual because it is fortified with a crenellated roof and battlements, reminding us that once Ibiza suffered from constant attacks by pirates, during which the villagers took refuge inside church.

Soon after passing San Jorge a sign to the left indicates Las Salinas and La Canal. This is a quiet minor road going south along flat countryside without habitation, until you come to the tiny village of **San Francisco,** which consists of one church, two houses, one bar, a football ground and twelve inhabitants — a bit different from the city of the same name in America! The **Church of San Francisco de Paula** was built in the late seventeenth century for the numerous workers from the salt pans, but it is now little used though well looked after.

Beyond San Francisco are the salt lakes of **Las Salinas** covering nearly one thousand acres at just below sea level, a shining scene of wet salt pans and pyramids of glistening white salt crystals. It was this precious commodity that, since the time of the Carthaginian colonists, attracted traders from other countries, perhaps helping the Ibicencos to develop their easy tolerance of foreigners. Until recently salt was the mainstay of the island economy, giving way to tourism only in the last decade. Even so some 60,000 tons of high grade sea salt is still exported each year — that is a lot of salt.

If you have never seen salt pans before it will be an interesting experience for you. Look at the various stages of evaporation of the sea water under the hot sunshine, from which salt is then collected and transported by a little train to waiting barges that lie alongside the docks at **La Canal,** the end of the road three kilometres on.

There is a small guesthouse, Hostal Las Salinas, set back off the road, a quiet place to stay except at weekends and holiday times when the restaurant becomes popular with Ibicencos who drive out from Ibiza town. Here a line of low pine woods and sand dunes form some shade and shelter from the hot sunshine that pours down on the wide stretch of Las Salinas beach; its lovely soft sloping sands have sunbeds and pedalos, and it is a good place for a picnic. You can swim, windsurf and walk, too, taking binoculars to observe the bird life.

If you are a keen naturist you are just a few kilometres west of Ibiza's official nudist beach of **Es Cavallet,** which has a wild natural setting of sand dunes, a long stretch of sand and fine pebbles. Reached by car, it has a large car park, beach bars and a restaurant where the prices are comparatively high.

In and around San José

Return along the road from La Canal and go past the salt lakes again. There is a minor road which allows you to take a short cut and join the main road to the airport. As you drive past the airport observe the attractive restored windmill there; in the past farmers were very dependent on these windmills for water supplies here in this flat arid land. Past the airport entrance the road turns north and along here, lying back off the road, is the **Camel Cellar.** Yes, there are several camels grazing in a field and, after leaving your car or coach in the park, you can walk across a track to a small shelter where two of these huge creatures are tethered and muzzled. A swift photographer takes your picture as you pose by these ships of the desert. Afterwards you are invited into a splendid old farmhouse cum wine cellar, where you can have as many free samples of liqueurs, spirits and wines as you wish, and after which the proprietor hopes you will purchase several bottles. Perhaps more interesting for some will be the old entrance hall with its faded pictures and old beams. Incidentally the ladies loo is the original, with old furnishings and bath.

On with the tour: the same road passes more old windmills, almond trees and fields as you join the main Ibiza town to San José road. In two kilometres there is a turn off to the left to visit the **Cova Santa** (Holy Cave). The story goes that the landowner was digging the ground to find a well, when he suddenly came upon this deep cave full of wonderful formations of stalactites and stalagmites. It is forty metres deep and over two hundred metres long — there are in fact two caves which are now well illuminated, and the temperature is a steady 15°C. The story also tells of a sixteenth-century tunnel leading from the sea to the caves where pirates hid their treasure. Now there is a café and disco outside. Open from 0930 to 1330 and 1500 to 1900 hrs.

A most unusual statue of Saint Francis of Assisi has a pig at his feet. It is in the church of Es Cubells.

Fourteen kilometres west of Ibiza town is the municipality of **San José.** It comprises San José, San Augustin, San Jorge and San Francisco. San José is in fact the largest of the island villages and it has a large and lovely old white church, which is a 'must' for tourists to see. Even if sightseeing is not of much interest to you, it is suggested that a few minutes spared to see this eighteenth-century church will be worthwhile, especially if you have a guide to tell you all about it.

During the Spanish Civil War the church was badly looted and partially destroyed. Today you see a church recently restored by the devotion of the villagers of San José. Over the altar a statue of the Bleeding Christ has a gold crown, paid for by the ladies of the village who sold their gold wedding and engagement rings. Unusually, Christ is seen wearing a white skirt. To one side of the altar is a moving statue, the figure of Mary Weeping — her alabaster face has a small tear on the cheek. Dressed all in black, the Madonna is wearing clothes lovingly made by the women of San José. On the west side a further colourful statue shows a knight slaying a Moor.

Hung around the church walls are El Greco copies; of great interest is a two sided picture of the Saviour showing wounds on both sides of the body, the artist is unknown. By the entrance is a modern painting of the Garden of Eden.

Whilst in the village have a browse around the gift shops; one sells hand-made lace and embroidered cloths. These are expensive but it's a rare opportunity to buy such handicrafts. There is a supermarket, a bank and a Firestone garage in the centre of the village.

From San José there are several detours to be made. The first is by taking a road due south across the eastern densely wooded slopes of **Mount Atalaya** (475 m), Ibiza's highest mountain. Signposted Es Cubells, this pleasant country route takes you past fields and isolated farm houses, with here and there old windmills minus their sails now converted into modern villas. About six kilometres from San José you reach the sleepy little hamlet of **Es Cubells,** which is little more than a cluster of a few houses, two bar/restaurants and a very nice church, all on the edge of a high cliff top. A theological seminary is perched even higher in a really remote position. Here in Es Cubells the air is fresh and invigorating. The deep blue sea seen below beats against the rocks; the road winds its way in hairpin bends to sea level and then in steep gradients along the coast. After a meal or some refreshment take a walk round the Plaza P.Francesc Yquer, a peaceful square, by the solid buttresses of the church. Inside, this fortress church is simple. Newly made windows let in light, the Image of the Madonna in black has in her hand a delicate white lace handkerchief. A statue of St Francis of Assisi shows him holding a long staff with a small pig at his feet. But do not linger as you must return to San José to fit in the next stage of the tour to the southwest coast and Cala Vedella.

The turning for this is on the western outskirts of San José; it is signposted Atalaya (also called Sa Talaia). Mount Atalaya was the scene of a fearful air disaster in 1972, when in fog an aircraft carrying an Ibizan football team and supporters crashed into the mountainside. There were no survivors. A cemetery at **Ses Roques Altes** (the high rocks) now marks the spot. It is possible to drive up this mountain if you are prepared to have a very bumpy ride along an unmade rutted track. In clear weather there are panoramic views, even as far as the Spanish mainland.

Cala Vedella, Cala Bassa and other beaches

But your journey to Cala Vedella is on a good road through some wooded areas, then dry stony land as it sweeps towards the sea. A turning to the left goes to **Cala Carbo** and **Cala D'Hort,** along an unmade dirt road past small farms of olive, almond and fig trees. In the distance you have some good views of the impressive **Isla Vedra,** a rocky islet, (328km) looking like some fairy tale castle; its steep escarpment points high into the sky, and only seabirds, goats and lizards enjoy its barren rocks. If you want a closer look at Vedra you must continue your rough ride to Cala D'Hort, a small but pretty sandy cove.

Continuing along the good road to **Cala Vedella,** you reach a new *urbanización* with many modern villas and apartments amongst wooded hills. The bay is wide and filled with glorious sands, with shallow water at the sea edge, some breakers for surfing, and boats for hire. This is a lovely beach venue for all the family. You will get very friendly service from the beach bar, Kiosk Geroni, and an excellent meal at reasonable prices. Try the *pinchetos,* tender pork pieces cooked on a skewer and similar to kebabs.

A winding coastal road leads to a series of *calas,* some with steep access like **Cala Moli,** which is very picturesque. **Cala Tarida** has wild and natural scenery with some rocks as well as sand, and clean waters which allow for good swimming and wind surfing. As there is no shade take a hat and some cover against the midday sun.

Some of the road surface in this corner of Ibiza is not too good, so time must be allowed for slower travel. When you reach **Cala**

Bassa, Cala Conta, Port D'es Torrent and **Punta Pinet** you are on the edge of the Bay of San Antonio, where all the beaches are a holidaymaker's paradise and offer every type of facility associated with Mediterranean *playas*.

Out at sea the island of **Conjera** stands imposingly. Its automatic lighthouse sends a beam which is seen forty-eight kilometres away. Boats can moor at the island and it makes an interesting sea trip, especially in spring when the wild flowers are blooming. Great care must be taken when swimming there because of sea urchins that have sharp quills.

San Antonio

Should time be short when leaving Cala Vedella, it is quicker not to take the coast road but to return to San José and the main road to reach San Antonio. This will take you through the oldest village in Ibiza, **San Augustin,** where there is another ancient church and across the road an old watch tower which is now used as a private house.

Viewed from the surrounding hills, **Bahia San Antonio** presents an inviting panorama, for this wide bay and natural harbour lie at the edge of a fertile plain where oranges and lemons grow. Eucalyptus and pines mingle with fields of corn. At the water's edge is **San Antonio Abad,** once a small fishing village and now Ibiza's busiest holiday resort, with a skyline full of modern high rise hotels and apartment blocks. Nearby, luxury yachts are moored in the harbour. Called Portus Magnus by the Romans, it now takes its name from the tiny white washed fourteenth-century parish church, dedicated to the Abbot Saint Anthony, which is tucked away in the back streets, just off Calle San Vicente. It is quite a gem, with its Moorish-style courtyard and rounded arches.

All roads lead to the long seafront promenade which is the centre of San Antonio, the Paseo Maritimo, a boulevard full of flower beds and fountains. Tables and chairs set out under shady palm trees belong to the many cafés and restaurants. Coach car and bus parks are right here, so is the Tourist Office. This is where the small ferry boats compete for passengers, to take you across to the sandy beaches that line the bay. The western end of the harbour has busy docks where the large vehicle and passenger ferries arrive and depart for Denia, near Alicante in mainland Spain. There is an added pleasure in the evenings, for this beautiful bay is noted for its breathtaking sunsets which are reflected in the calm waters.

Cheerful San Antonio is the place for busy souvenir shops and a multitude of cafés, restaurants, music bars and discos. The town goes to bed very late (or is it early in the morning?) so here the hotels serve breakfast later and no one is on the streets before 0930 hrs.

Just where Calle Ramon Y Cajal intersects with Calle San Vicente, on the way to Can Germa, you cannot fail to see a huge stone statue of a man with his hands cupped to his mouth. This monument, *El Payes* (the farmer), was designed and sculptored by an Ibicenco, Antonio Hormigo. Larger than life, this Ibicenco countryman is depicted crying *'Uc'* — a cry heard only on Ibiza, which can be a sound of defiance and challenge, or of exuberance and exaltation. We like to think of it as a welcome! A second statue, by Sebastian Terasa, depicts a youthful barefoot sailor, with oars and a net flung over one shoulder; called *Hombre del Mar* (Man of the Sea) it stands at the intersection of Calle Balanzat and Calle Santa Innes, which is quite near the sea front.

To the northwest of San Antonio lie **Cala Gracio, Can Germa** and **Cap Negret,** more hotels and an opportunity for some low clifftop walks. A minor road leads up into the countryside and to **Santa Innes,** but for the purpose of the tour you must take another route.

Leaving the music and swinging crowds of San Antonio, you travel fast on the new modern highway to Ibiza town. At Km 11 is the glass blowing factory called **Castell D'es Puig,** interesting to watch, useful for presents and with a handy bar for refreshments. About half way between San Antonio and Ibiza town is the village of **San Rafael.** To reach it you must divert from the main road. From the plaza in front of the church is an unexpectedly fine view of Ibiza town and Dalt Vila; sometimes you can even see Formentera in the distance. Along the quiet main street of San Rafael are a few potters' houses, which are really cottage industries. You cannot be sure when these shops will be open, though you may like to purchase some ceramics.

Return to the main road again, the traffic increases as you near the town. On your left, on top off the small hill of **Monte Cristo,** is a huge statue of Christ with outstretched arms, a replica of one in Gran Rey, Brazil.

The tour finishes as you reach Ibiza town again, in the knowledge that the south and west of Ibiza offer a wonderful variety of scenery: white salt lakes, green pine forests, lemon and orange groves and always the blue and gold *calas,* where it is hard not to linger.

ELEVEN

Touring Ibiza: the north

This tour of the north of Ibiza begins and ends at Ibiza town and takes in Portinatx, San Miguel, Puerto de San Miguel, San Mateo and Santa Innes. Allow one full day for this trip of some 112 kms.

Ibiza town to Portinatx

With Ibiza town as the departure point, take the ring road out and head towards Santa Eulalia for about seven kilometres watching carefully for the road sign to San Juan and Portinatx. You are quickly into open countryside, green and scattered with typical Ibizan houses — squat, flat-roofed white cubes, so practical to extend by just adding another square room! Ibizan housewives are houseproud and every springtime they get out their brushes and paint the thick walls of their houses, doing so again in the summer if necessary. Here the fields are intensely cultivated, some with salad crops, others with corn and broad beans growing tall. Everywhere you see the sturdy dark green algarroba tree, with its long carob beans which were so important to the islanders during the 1936 Spanish Civil War; food was then so desperately short that this bean had to provide sustenance for both man and beast.

Now the roadside has many wild flowers and the hills are covered with heather and pine trees, the air is sweet with many herbs. There is little traffic on the road; the few wayside bars and restaurants will be busy in the middle of the day and during evenings. Near the village of **San Lorenzo** you see set on low hills several round watch towers, a reminder that Ibiza's past is a history of constant invasion. The tiny fortified village of **Balafi** has a distinct Moorish flavour and if time permits do wander along its quiet, narrow cobbled streets.

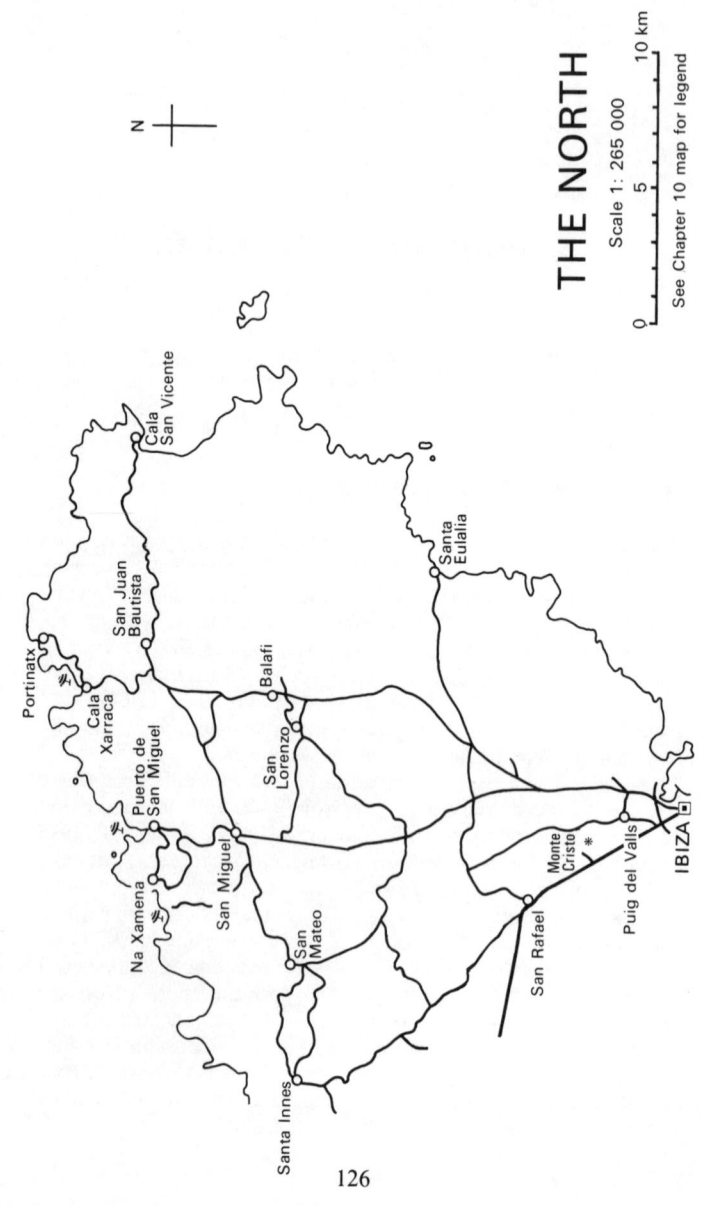

Travelling on towards the north the road is undulating and at times the surface is only fair, so do not drive too fast. Just past **Sa Taulera** a left turn goes to San Miguel but continue on northwards for a short distance then turn left to Portinatx. On the outskirts of **San Juan** is the only petrol station in the area, so check your petrol gauge, tyres and oil level.

Now the adventurous drive high into the mountains begins, for the road to Portinatx has at least thirty-four bends, some being quite sharp. (The courier on coach excursions warns nervous tourists to close their eyes, that is what their driver does!) It really is a splendid mountain route through dense pine forests; in places trees have been cleared so that luxurious modern villas perched on an escarpment have marvellous views across the island and sea. Well known people like Jackie Onassis, Niki Lauda and Terry Thomas have built properties in this part of Ibiza.

The road finally reaches the coast at **Cala Xarraca,** an amazing cove locked in by high cliffs; the turquoise waters below are wonderfully translucent and calm, ideal for snorkelling. The series of small sandy coves that make up **Portinatx** are so beautiful that part of the film *South Pacific* was shot on a beach here. Another claim to fame is that during Spanish naval exercises in 1929, King Alfonso XIII came ashore here; immediately the beach was officially named Portinatx del Rey.

How nice to have your meal overlooking the sea, at Playa Portinatx.

There is plenty of car parking space before you reach the end of the road. Buses from Ibiza town and Santa Eulalia arrive through the day and island tour coaches usually stay here for about three hours. Hence the variety of souvenir shops.

Hotels and apartment blocks are rising fast and the area is becoming popular, especially with the British tourists who appreciate this quiet resort with beautiful scenery and golden sands. Sufficient small supermarkets cater for visitors but there is no nightlife, except that which is provided in the hotels. The energetic will enjoy a walk in the pinewoods (be careful not to get lost amongst the many pathways that all look alike) but the ground is dry, hard, stony and sometimes slippery, so sturdy footwear is required. Down on the beach there is a sub-aqua school and beach bars. Pedalos and sunbeds can be hired. This is a lovely beach for toddlers as the water's edge is very shallow and warm, just the place for sand castles.

In and around San Miguel

To continue the tour it is necessary to retrace the route from Portinatx to San Juan, then back to the turning off the main road to San Miguel, which is about seven kilometres further on. The large white fourteenth-century church on a hill top in **San Miguel**, dominates the countryside. This cruciform edifice is graced with black and white frescoes; in the courtyard are several old relics such as an old wine press. Rather incongruously there is a letter box in the wall by the entrance to the church, and the post office (*correos*) is in the adjacent bar.

Outside in the courtyard, every Thursday during the tourist season, there is folk music and dancing. Champagne is served at 150 pesetas (£0.68). It is suggested that you leave your car parked in the main street below and walk the short distance to the church, as part of the road is narrow and one-way.

The view from the top, looking out over the countryside to the sea, gives a wide vista of the north of Ibiza. A service is held in the church every Sunday at 1030 hrs; tourists are welcome.

Having reached San Miguel it is worthwhile travelling a further four kilometres to **Puerto de San Miguel** (Port St Miguel). This is a natural deep water harbour that lies at the end of a narrow fertile valley. With steep limestone cliffs on each side of the bay, the sandy beach is sheltered and good for family swimming. Boat excursions,

The fine Church of San Miguel, 14th century. Here in the courtyard exhibitions of folk music and dancing can be enjoyed during the tourist season.

The thick pine forests, turquoise waters and golden sands are seen here at Puerto San Miguel in the north of Ibiza.

wind surfing, pedalos and water-ski can be enjoyed and lay-out chairs are for hire on the beach. A bus service runs between here and Ibiza town.

Small fishing boats bring in fish daily, including lobsters. These are served in the local restaurants. High on one side of the cliffs two large hotels have been constructed — some say to the detriment of the landscape, although the hotel visitors would not agree as they have a splendid position. This is a pleasant spot for walking; you can also visit the **Cuevas de Can Marca** (open at 1030 hrs) that are along the road high up the mountain behind the Galeon Hotel. A rough unmade road leads to the entrance. There is a car park and bar. Multi lingual tours start every hour. Inside the cave has good lighting and sound effects which enhance this fascinating world of pillars, pools, stalagmites and stalactites.

Whilst in this part of Ibiza you may care to take a short drive to **Na Xamena** where, tucked away in really thick pine woods, is the exclusive four-star Hotel Hacienda, set in delightful tropical gardens on the edge of the cliffs. It has an out of this world setting, so idyllic and peaceful. Barbecue meals are served on the patio by the pool; at night all is beautifully floodlit.

San Mateo and Santa Innes

As the hotel is at the end of the road it is necessary to backtrack to the road leading to San Miguel. Back in the village take the direction south, which will pass isolated houses set back from the road, with the surrounding land being well cultivated. In about five kilometres you can turn right on to a minor road that leads to the remote village of San Mateo; or you can continue on to Santa Gertrudis using a better road.

Santa Gertrudis is a small peaceful village which these days is notable as the departure point of the Donkey Trek. More than fifty trained donkeys (*burros*) work at the ranch, taking squealing passengers on a ride into the mountains, to be followed by wine tasting, food and games, then — even more hilarious — the journey homewards.

On the road to San Mateo, if you are a country lover, then you will drive slowly to enjoy this quiet rural atmosphere, where sheep and goats graze peacefully and flocks of pigeons fly low over cornfields. If you happen to see anyone working in the fields or gathering olives from the trees give a wave. Their work is arduous and they look upon tourists with friendly curiosity. However, do not be surprised if the old lady in black turns her head away from your camera, the old folk are intensely superstitious and still believe in evil spirits, hanging up strings of garlic at their front door to keep away devils. They will never be found sitting under a Judas tree (*Cercis Siliquastrum*) because in the past that was the tree used to hang pirates.

As you approach **San Mateo** the road deteriorates into a dirt track until you finally reach the little white church, passing, on the way, the Stations of the Cross which lead to the church doors. In the past this church was used both for worship and as a fortress in times of attacks by pirates — as with most churches on the island. Today you notice that the priest's house, which is built as part of the church, does not have a cannon on top, but just a TV aerial!

If you wish to see yet more of these isolated little villages, then return down the road you came on for about four kilometres, and look for a rather faded road sign to Santa Innes (or maybe it is now Santa Agnes), which is a further seven kilometres northwest. Along here there are more remote farms with goats, pigs and sheep, note how the animals are hobbled to keep them from straying, as there are few proper fences. In springtime the almond blossom creates a pink and white haze over the fields; the rest of the year it is the silver grey foliage and twisted trunks of olive trees that catch the eye. Some vines are grown in this area, but the wine is only for local consumption. Probably you will drive along this country way and never see another vehicle, nor even a bicycle, for you are now well off the tourist routes.

Santa Innes, apart from the aforementioned farm houses, consists of two nice little bar/restaurants and the church. It is Ibiza's most remote village. This makes a restful stopping place for refreshments and here the bill will not strain your pocket.

On the homeward journey it is possible to take a minor road across the top of the mountain westwards, giving views of the offshore islands, and then drop down into the back streets of San Antonio. But do not make for the **Cuevas de las Fontanellas,** without first finding out from the Tourist Office if they are open. At the time of writing they have been closed as being too dangerous for visitors.

Having already visited San Antonio (Chapter Ten) we take the road from Santa Innes which leads directly to San Rafael (see Chapter Ten) where there are bars and restaurants for typical Ibizan food. The Grill San Rafael, next to the hilltop church, has lovely terraces and a gracious beamed dining room. The international menu has the distinction of being the only one in Ibiza recommended in the famous Gourmettour Guide. Open for lunch and dinner, this is the place for a special meal. The Hippodrome is here too, where on a Sunday afternoon you can see trotting races, and food and drink is available.

We are nearing the end of today's journey into the beautiful countryside of Ibiza, where one is never without the fragrant aroma of herbs. Near the village of **Puig D'en Valls,** a few kilometres north of Ibiza town, is the modern distillery of the Mari Mayans family. Founded in 1880, this is the place where the distinctive liqueurs of Ibiza are made. Great grandfather Mari started the business on Formentera making Frigola, from the purple flowering thyme that grows on the island, and Hierbas Ibicencas, from a selection of natural herbs; but he had to move to Ibiza because of shipping problems.

The distillery uses sixteen different herbs, all native to the islands, but the recipes are a closely guarded secret. Some of the most common herbs used are fennel, rosemary, verbena and aniseed. One of the nice things about buying these liqueurs is that after enjoying the different flavours, you still have the attractive bottles. Some are replicas of Ibizan country people in typical dress; another is an accurate copy of the statue of the ancient goddess Tanit, one of Ibiza's archaeological treasures. They make a nice reminder of your holiday.

Full of sweet country air, you are soon back again in Ibiza town. It will take a few moments to adjust again to the pace of modern life.

A pastoral scene along the road between San Mateo and Santa Innes, where the land is well cultivated.

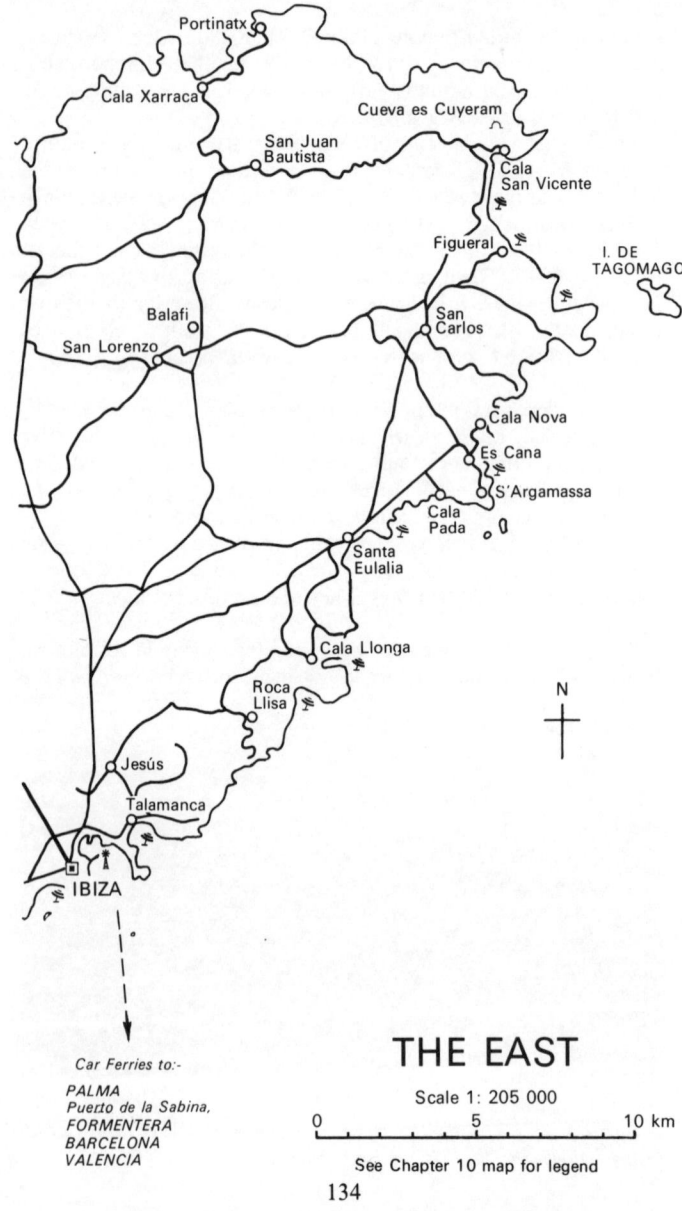

TWELVE

Touring Ibiza: the east

Ibiza town is again the starting and finishing point for this tour of the east of the island, which takes in Jesús, Cala Llonga, Santa Eulalia, Es Cana, Punta Arabi, San Carlos, Cala San Vicente and San Juan. It will take one full day for the tour, which is some 72 km.

Jesús and Cala Llonga

Leave Ibiza town along the Avenida de Santa Eulalia, the road that runs along the port with the Casino on your left. Shortly you arrive at the mini holiday resort of Talamanca, situated on a promontory to the east of the great harbour. From here you see a fine view of Dalt Vila; early in the morning or at twilight it has an outstanding silhouette against the clear skies. The curved sandy beach of Talamanca is popular with water-ski and wind surfing enthusiasts who stay in the various hotels and apartments that line the water's edge. There is little shade on this beach. It is a convenient place for anyone interested in being near Ibiza town, yet wishing to avoid the late night crowds and can be reached by bus or ferry.

From Talamanca a road leads to the small village of **Jesús.** No tourists stay here but they do come to visit the fifteenth-century church and admire a valuable piece of Gothic art, the Triptych from the fifteenth-century Valencian school of Rodrigo de Osuna, which hangs over the altar. The central panel depicting the Virgin and Child is surrounded by supporting panels with pictures of the Apostles. Beneath these panels is a sequence of seven scenes relating to the Virgin's life. Like many rural churches this one is often closed. Almost opposite the church are shops that include a large supermarket and, nearby a butcher's (*carnicera*) with very good fresh meat.

Between Jesús and Cala Llonga the land rises sharply and is deeply wooded; it is here on a high plateau that you find Ibiza's only golf course (nine-hole) at **Roca Llisa.**

The road twists and turns until it drops down into the valley and regains sea level at **Cala Llonga.** This magnificent wide sandy beach is very attractive with pine clad hills either side. Here are large hotels and holiday apartments, a few shops, restaurant and cafés. The sheltered beach has shallow water that shelves gently, making it just right for families with young children. Wind surfing, snorkelling, pedalos and fishing are popular sports. At nights there is plenty of entertainment in the hotels. The Wild Asparagas is a reputable venue that has a good international menu and at night the tables are set beneath lanterns near the floodlit swimming pool — a romantic setting overlooking the bay.

Santa Eulalia del Rio

Continue on this road, joining with the main Ibiza town to Santa Eulalia road. The road in to the town crosses the bridge over the only river in the Balearic Islands. But do not expect a fast-flowing expanse of water, except in the rainy season; most of the time it is only a light trickle. Parallel with this bridge is a low arched and cobbled bridge, said to be of Roman construction, but there is a local legend that it was built in one night by the Devil himself!

Santa Eulalia del Rio is the second most populated town, and one of the first places on the island to attract foreign artists and writers. In the past Santa Eulalia was primarily a market centre and even today much of the island produce arrives for further distribution. There is a daily market for the people of Santa Eulalia.

Despite the fact that it has very little beach the town has, over the last ten years, expanded beyond all recognition. Large apartment blocks and tourist hotels are being built in great density; recently a large new yacht marina has taken shape and no doubt will soon be full of expensive luxury yachts. A new promenade, the Paseo Maritimo, with landscaped gardens, is under construction. Lined with modern apartments, it also has a good selection of restaurants. It is a pleasant place for a seaside stroll.

Tree lined Calle San Jaime separates the old part of the town from the new, which is seawards. The old Town Hall (*Ayuntamiento*) is at the top of the small main square, the Plaza España, which has ornate fountains, palm trees and a memorial to the brave people of Santa Eulalia who rescued survivors from the

S.A. Mallorca shipwrecked in 1913. Around the square cafés and bars are always busy; it is the central meeting place for families and friends. Across Calle San Jaime is the Paseo S'Alamera which leads down to the sea; here are tall trees, colourful oleanders and hibiscus. Street vendors and instant portrait artists make this a lively scene. There is some car parking but mainly the space is for the taxi rank on the east of the Paseo, in Calle G. Franco. There are bus stops and shops, bars and telephones — the latter manned by a telephonist who will assist in obtaining international calls for a small fee. On the west side of the Paseo in Calle Mariano Riquer is the Tourist Office and another bus stop. There are plenty of tourist shops in Santa Eulalia and it is a good place to look for handmade clothes and lace tablecloths.

If you are looking for paintings and sculptures, Galeria El Mensajero in Calle Isidoro Macabich 32, is open from 1030 to 1300 and 1700 to 2000 hrs. There is a chemist (*farmacia*) in this street also. Here, too, is an attractive little square with a 1983 statue called *Homenaje a Pagesa* (Homage to the Peasant) plus some lovely old brass cannon dated 1605.

Nuestra Senora de Jesús, 14th century church stands in the original hilltop village of Santa Eulalia.

In summer, ferry boats operate a daily service between Santa Eulalia and the beaches of Cala Padua, Es Cana and Cala Llonga, first departure 0930 hrs.

Most visitors to Santa Eulalia want to know about its hill top fourteenth-century church Nuestra Señora de Jesús. It is an outstanding landmark and can be seen from afar. To reach the Puig de la Missa (Hill of the Mass) you have a stiff walk up, or you can drive to the top where parking is limited; taking a taxi is a good idea. The return is an easy walk, down hill. The Puig de la Missa is the oldest part of the town and quite the most attractive with its tiny narrow streets and cube-shaped houses full of pretty flowers.

Crowned by its white church, which was built originally in 1568 over a Mosque and dedicated to Santa Eulalia, the church has an attractive flagstone courtyard with arched pillars. Inside is a wooden ornate altar screen, a Gothic rerados, carved in the fifteenth century. Much of the church treasure was lost during the Spanish Civil War when part of the church was destroyed by fire. There are two services in Spanish on Sundays, at 0930 and 2000 hrs. Next door to the church is a small museum, Museo Barrau, which contains a collection of paintings by the impressionist Catalan artist, Barrau.

From the top of Puig de la Missa there are wonderful panoramic views of Santa Eulalia, the surrounding green countryside, the coast line and far out to sea, making it worth the effort to get there.

Es Cana and Punta Arabi

Leaving Santa Eulalia, continue on the road that bears right to Es Cana. If you are looking for a bar resaurant, out of town, try Es Farallo, Carretera Es Cana, Km 1. Tel: 33 07 85. This typically Ibizan low building has an old olive tree and creeping plants outside, where you can sit and have a drink. Inside you will enjoy fresh fish and meats well prepared. This establishment is recommended by the Tourist Office in Santa Eulalia.

The country is flat here with some large hotels near the coast by **S'Argamassa.** The sandy beach is safe for children and has facilities for water sports. There is also horse riding and pleasant pine woods for walking. The area is ideal for bicycle rides; most hotels have them for hire.

Next along this road we reach **Cala Pada** and another sandy beach good for water sports; there is a Diving School here and a beach bar. The road continues to wind through the pleasant

Sailing boats of various sizes can be hired by the day or hour. Seen here at Es Cana.

countryside where olive trees and vegetables are grown, until it reaches **Es Cana,** which in recent years has developed into a thriving little resort.

Numerous hotels lie along the front sheltered by pine trees and the natural curve of the bay. A friendly place, it has a wide arc of pale sand, lovely for children as well as water sports enthusiasts. Restaurants, cafés, supermarkets and souvenir shops line the streets. Bars and discothèques supplement entertainments in the hotels.

Sea excursions from Es Cana go to the nearby Isla de Tagomago, the further islet of Espalmador, and Formentera. An all-day cruise stopping for a swim costs about 2,350 pesetas (£10.60). The ferry from Es Cana to Santa Eulalia takes twenty-five minutes and runs throughout the day, costing 250 pesetas (£1.13). This is a good area for walking along dusty roads and through pinewoods to sandy beaches such as **Cala Nova** and **Cala Llena,** stopping at hotels for refreshments. Cala Nova has wild and pretty scenery, with a large stretch of sand; sometimes the breakers are strong and an under tow makes it dangerous for swimming. There are two Camping Sites near Es Cana.

Within walking distance, if you are fit, is **Punta Arabi** which is a holiday complex of apartments. It is here that the well-known Hippy Market is held every Wednesday. It's very much a tourist attraction, though these days there are not many genuine 'hippies', but more gipsy vendors from Andulusia; it is a cheerful outing to join the crowds, some of the paintings and craft work are original, others may have come from China or Hong Kong.

San Carlos

Leaving Es Cana and its outlying villas and driving northwards to San Carlos, you wind through the principal agricultural areas of Ibiza. Here are fields of corn and golden sun flowers, lines of cabbages, lettuces and artichokes, and always the sturdy thick white walls of the Ibizan *finca* with bright flowers round the door, an outside baking oven and watchful guard dog. No wonder so many artists and writers decide to settle in this tranquil setting.

San Carlos is renowned for its Bohemian atmosphere and, of course, the fine white church built in the eighteenth century. Restaurants and bars have outdoor tables, so just the place for a drink and a chat. A well-known restaurant and discothèque is Las Dalias, on the Santa Eulalia road. San Carlos is an important junction. From here you can turn inland across the **Morna Valley,** so beautiful in almond blossom time, but this tour continues up the coast.

At Es Cana this restaurant has special menu's for children. Most other resorts will have similar places.

Cala San Vicente and San Juan

In the centre of the village turn left and take the road to Cala San Vicente; quickly it starts to climb, curving through lush green forests and then along the top of cliffs, giving a splendid view of the whale-like **Isla de Tagomago.** It is an exhilarating drive with some uneven surfaces.

There are turnings seawards for **Es Figueral** and **S'Aigua Blanca.** The latter has the unofficial reputation for being a place to get an overall tan and it certainly has some peaceful spots. Es Figueral, reached down a winding road, lies about eleven kilometres north of Santa Eulalia, to which it is connected by bus. Pine woods back this narrow beach, where facilities include watersports, bar/restaurants, cafés and apartments.

Just before you reach **Cala San Vicente** you will have a most marvellous view of the bay from the cliff top road. You are sure to want to stop to take a photograph, but be careful of traffic for there is little space to park a vehicle. So you drop down quickly to sea level and turn seawards to this remote resort. Swimming can be difficult here owing to the breakers and undertow. The Germans seem to favour this development, it is noticeable that restaurants show menus in German rather than English. There are good fish restaurants right by the beach, which is pebble and sand.

The Restaurant Can Miguel serves meals outside as well as inside. The menu includes roast chicken 300 pesetas (£1.36), entrecote 600 pesetas (£2.72), red mullet 500 pesetas (£2.27), Spanish omelet 225 pesetas (£1.05). There is a large car park in the middle of the village.

Behind the beach and hotels is an unmade road that winds very steeply up the side of the cliff to **Cueva Es Cuyeram** (the caves) where Carthaginian relics, including several replicas of the famous figure the Moon Goddess Tanit, were discovered in a temple.

From Cala Vicente we take another lovely mountain drive to the village of **San Juan Bautista.** On the outskirts are several steep gradients between the thick woods. Look out for the rare Elenora's falcon and the golden eagles that soar over these mountains. San Juan, twenty-two kilometres from Ibiza, is a peaceful place with most of the population living on scattered farms and only coming into the village to do business. It must be mentioned that on the outskirts of San Juan is the only petrol station in these parts.

Westwards from San Juan the road joins with the main Portinatx to Ibiza town road which has been described in chapter 11. If time allows on your return journey, you can make a detour to visit **Perlas Orquidea,** the Majorca Pearl Showrooms, which are situated halfway between Santa Eulalia and Ibiza town. They are easy to locate by the big sign and international flags, near the large car park. Inside is a small display showing how these pearls are manufactured. Showcases display a wide selection of pearl jewellery which can be purchased. Other souvenirs include olive wood, ceramics, musical boxes and ornaments, all easy to pack gifts.

THIRTEEN
Formentera

The Romans called this island Frumentaria, which signified an abundance of wheat. Later the name became Forment, the Catalan word for wheat, and from this comes the current name of Formentera. It seems hard to believe that this little island ever produced sufficient wheat to send to the soldiers in Ibiza. Most of the soil is now barren and dry; few trees grow except on the higher ground of La Mola. However, today's holidaymakers do not complain about the lack of wheat or vegetation, they just delight in Formentera's lovely blue skies, warm seas and golden sands.

To reach the island you must travel by boat as there is no airport. There is a service from mainland Spain: from Denia, near Alicante, the ferry goes direct to Puerto La Sabina, Formentera. But the majority of visitors take the ferry from Ibiza town harbour which is about eighteen kilometres from Puerto La Sabina. Many others make day excursions from San Antonio, Santa Eulalia and Es Cana.

The tour of the island described here is about 75 km and it may be made as a full day excursion from Ibiza, though it is easily adapted if you are spending more time on Formentera. The main places covered by the tour are Puerto La Sabina, San Francisco Javier, Cala Sahona, Cala Berberia, San Fernando, Es Pujols, Playa Mitjorn, Playa Es Arenal, Es Calo, La Mola and Las Salinas.

Ibiza town to Puerto La Sabina

It is suggested that you leave early in the morning from Ibiza town for your tour of Formentera. Do choose a day when the weather is fine, for the crossing can be rough at times. It is sensible not to make the excursion the day before your return flight to the UK

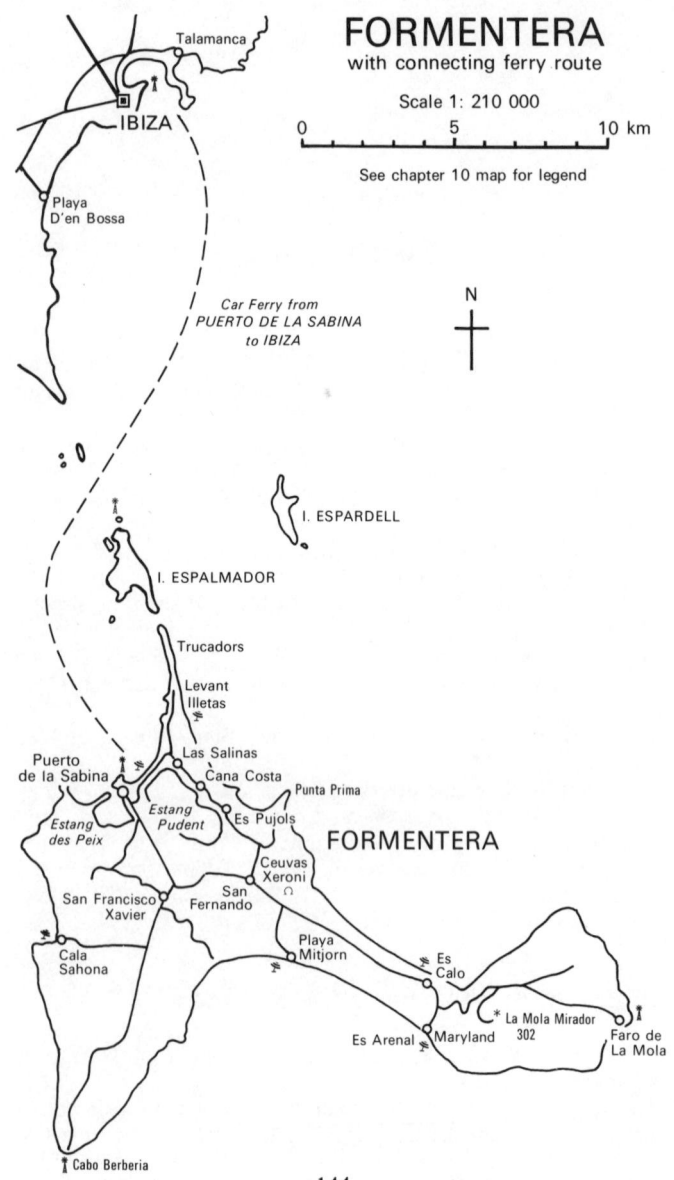

since, if it becomes very windy and rough, there is a risk that the return ferry to Ibiza will be delayed until the next day. The sea crossing takes about one hour, slightly longer if you use the vehicle ferry, which travels more slowly.

Sailing out of Ibiza port the view of the old city and harbours is magnificent. High above the modern town is Dalt Vila, with its great bastion walls, mighty cathedral and castle, standing guardian over the island. As you leave the southern tip of Ibiza, into view comes the island of **Vedra,** another imposing sight, for its craggy rocks and cliffs jut up from sea level to 328m and are the haunt of wild birds, flowers and goats.

Next you sail close to the islet of **Ahorcados,** locally called Hang Island, because, in times past this is where captured pirates were hanged and then left to rot, as a fearful warning to other corsairs. A much nicer story is associated with the next sandy islet that is passed, **Espalmador** which lies nearer to Formentera: the last owner died a few years ago and in his will he declared the island a nature reserve. Nowadays only a caretaker lives there looking after the fifty-two fig trees that still thrive. Yachts like to shelter in the sandy bay and beach parties arrive by boat to picnic. You can climb up the sand dunes to look at the old ruined watchtower on the low, red sandstone cliffs.

On arrival at **Puerto La Sabina,** Formentera's newly enlarged port, you see only the modern buildings of the port authorities and some new apartments. Here you may rent a car, bicycle or moped. If you are fortunate you may find a taxi available or catch the bright orange coloured bus. Much is made in tourist publicity of the suitability of exploring the island by bicycle, for it is only ninety kilometres in length. Some of the bicycles have small pillion seats for young children.

One main road leads out of La Sabina and soon you reach the only petrol filling station on Formentera, which closes at dusk. On either side of the road are two lagoons, the smaller one, **Estanq des Peix** (lagoon of the fish) has small boats and yachts moored and is said to be a wonderful place for fishing because the spawn is trapped there. The larger lagoon is **Estanq Pudent** (the stinking lagoon), it being a dead water pond.

San Francisco Javier

It is just two kilometres to the capital **San Francisco Javier;** watch out that you do not miss the turning for the centre of town, there is no sign but it is by a small cluster of shops, one of which is the only chemist's (*farmacia*) on the island. Driving up the main street you will pass on your right the Town Hall, the Tourist Office and Health Centre.

All too quickly you are in the central square, feeling that you have stepped back many years in time. Here stands the solid eighteenth-century Church of San Francisco. Bare of any exterior adornment, its white-washed stone is reminiscent of North Africa. It was built as a refuge for the islanders from marauding pirates, when the entire inhabitants and their livestock would lock themselves inside this fortress church, staying there until their unwelcome visitors had left empty-handed. Even today the church interior is dark, having only two tiny windows. One painting on the wall is a colourful mural, the work of a local artist, showing Christ baptising John the Baptist.

Coming out of the cool church, your eyes will blink in the bright sunshine. Across the road you see Pepe's Fonda Bar, Formentera's oldest bar and worth a visit. Sometimes a few 'hippy' types put up stalls in the Plaza; no one seems to mind this free trading and some of the hand-made jewellery is quite attractive.

The three main streets in the capital have a fair share of souvenir shops and several sell jumpers and cardigans made from the thick wool from the local sheep. These garments feel quite coarse and heavy, but they are a protection against the strong winds that blow here in the winter especially. It is possible to buy hanks of this wool, should you wish to knit your own garment; the natural wool is dyed in pleasant muted colours of grey, blue, green, pink and brown.

When you are looking for somewhere to eat, the Hostal Can Rafal has a clean restaurant, the menu of the day offers a three-course meal for about 550 pesetas (£2.50). Or you can order such dishes as a French omelet 150 pesetas (£0.63), tunny fish salad 350 pesetas (£1.59) or pork chop 400 pesetas (£1.82).

Cala Sahona and Cabo Berberia

A side road leading from the scattered capital goes southwest towards one of Formentera's principal heights, **Puig Guillem** (107m). A turning west along a narrow road leads three kilometres to **Cala Sahona.** Here is just one pleasant *hostal,* a few apartments and a restaurant plus a sandy beach with lovely clear waters; there are no other facilities on this undeveloped shore.

The countryside is only sparsely scattered with buildings; most of the fields have dry stone walls, though near the capital these hand laid walls are gradually being replaced with walls built of concrete blocks, which are really ugly. Several old windmills improve the scenery and here many fig trees are so enormous that the spreading branches have to be propped up with poles; these also protect them from the strong winds. Their owners like to sit under the shade of these trees at siesta time.

Returning to the road leading to San Francisco Javier, you can turn right and take a bumpy drive on the track to **Cabo Berberia**, where there's an old watch tower called El Torre des Cap. The land down here is dreadfully bare, dry and dusty from the cruel Tramontana winds, and only a few wild goats survive. So do not linger but return again to **San Francisco Javier** and here turn right on to the main road and it is just three kilometres to San Fernando.

San Fernando, Es Pujols and the Caves of Xeroni

The small village of **San Fernando** has a few shops, bar restaurants, a church and a supermarket — but nothing special for visitors. However, it does have the road that leads down to the sea at **Es Pujols**, which is the main tourist resort in Formentera. Do not expect much in the way of entertainment or facilities even here, for this tiny island still remains mostly undeveloped.

Es Pujols consists of a number of new apartment blocks, supermarkets and supporting shops; outside the bar restaurants the menus are in German. There seems to have been little planning, so everywhere is a hotchpotch of unfinished projects and half-built premises. This is where, close to the beach, coach excursions from Ibiza disgorge their passengers with a 'there's the beach' attitude. After reading some of the tourist and package holiday descriptions, some may frankly be disappointed with the beach at Es Pujols, whilst others settle happily on the white sands or sit in the beach bars having a meal and a chat. Along a narrow sandy shore children play happily, but beware of seaweed and tar which can get on clothes and shoes.

The reflection of the sun and sky on the clear seas creates a marvellous colour effect of shades of aquamarine and turquoise which will make you reach for your camera. Here the light reflecting off the white buildings is very strong; where possible a faster shutter speed is required. The shops here have popular sized films like Kodak, usually costing about twice the UK price. Spanish Negra and Valca films are cheaper and good enough for ordinary

White, white sands and shallow water at Es Pujols make it the most popular resort for coach tours.

snapshots. Printing and developing takes about one to three days.

While at Es Pujols enjoy a walk along the beach; at one end is a row of old fishing huts with ancient wooden slipways, while the other way sand dunes and low pine trees make a contrasting picture. Farther on at **Punta Prima** is an old watch tower.

When you feel that you have had sufficient of the beach, make a visit to **Cuevas Xeroni**, caves that are reached a short distance off the main road, one kilometre south of San Fernando. They are not difficult to locate for opposite is a large supermarket called Ofiusa. This cave is one of the most interesting places to visit on the island. Although quite small it has very good examples of stalagmites and stalactites which, with clever lighting effects, cause the mind to think of fairy tales and magical lands. At the entrance is a small bar. Admission to the cave is 75 pesetas (£0.34).

Playa Mitjorn and Playa Es Arenal

To continue the tour of Formentera now drive along the most narrow part of the island, a small isthmus just two kilometres from shore to shore. A turning to the right leads down a short lane to **Playa Mitjorn.** This is the famous white sandy beach that stretches for about six kilometres. In the centre is the large Hotel Formentera which offers every comfort and a wonderful location right at the edge of this (so far) unspoilt beach, where sweet scented pines offer some shade and topless and nude swimming is the norm.

It is necessary to return to the main road to reach the next access place. Again it is down a dusty unmade track to **Playa Es Arenal.** There's one *finca* (farmhouse) and a *hostal,* and you walk through the pines to this 'away from it all' beach. Take your own cover up and lots of sun tan lotion. Close to this beach is the development called **Hotel Club Maryland** — an informal holiday complex of bungalows built in a park-like setting, right at the edge of the beach. It offers lots of activities, sports, dancing, discos, fashion shows and video in English, and is good value for a family holiday.

More luxurious is the Ibertol four-star hotel Club La Mola, where you have a choice of hotel or bungalow accommodation right by the sea. Honeymoon couples get a free bottle of bubbly and fruit on arrival. Adults celebrate birthdays with a gala dinner.

Es Calo to Faro de La Mola

Back to the tour: continuing south we pass the cluster of houses that comprise Es Calo, where the tiny harbour dates back to Roman times, when it was the only port in the island. Gradually it is being developed with apartments for today's tourists. From here the road rises sharply and on either side the green vegetation makes a welcome respite for the eyes.

This is **La Mola** (192m) the highest point. A viewing point (*mirador*) allows visitors to enjoy a spectacular panorama of the entire northern areas of Formentera and way beyond to the little islets and Ibiza. Looking across the green pines to the road you have just travelled, you can see the glorious sandy beaches on either side; it is a breathtaking and memorable sight.

Having gazed your fill, you can enjoy some refreshment at the bar of El Mirador. Be sure to taste the fig bread (*pan de higo*); it is very sustaining because it contains chopped almonds as well as figs. Another speciality here is the goat's cheese and honey cake.

There is only one more village to pass through and, if it were not for the little white church, you might miss **Nuestra Senora del Pilar** altogether, for the houses around are very few and scattered. Here on this high plateau a few sheep and cattle graze; some low growing vines are seen behind stone walls. Formentera's red wine (*vino pahés*) has a distinctive dry flavour but not sufficient is produced for it to be exported.

The road continues on to the easternmost tip of the land and the tall lighthouse, **Faro de La Mola,** built in 1861. Steep cliffs prevent any swimming and the bare flat landscape is quite desolate. A monument commemorates the fact that the Faro de La Mola figures in the Jules Verne story *Journey Round the Solar System.* That and a small bar and souvenir shop are all that is to be seen here on this windswept expanse of land.

On your return journey you may wish to stop and photograph one lone and rather magnificent windmill with long vanes, which stands out a short walk from the road way. This striking picture is shown in much of the tourist publicity.

Las Salinas and nearby beaches

Another interesting place to visit is Formentera's ancient salt pans, called **Las Salinas,** reputed to yield about 20,000 tons of salt each year. These salt pans have been in use since Roman times and the

This magnificent old windmill is one of Formentera's outstanding landmarks on the road to Cabo Mola.

density of the salt crystals is higher than in Ibiza. To reach the salt lakes you need to drive to the outskirts of La Sabina, then turn right eastwards down a rough lane. Drive to the end and do not despair, you are not lost, because you turn left and there before you are the salt pans, the white crystals standing out vividly like soap suds on the shining water. A sandy track now winds along a narrow strip of land with the sea very close. Amongst the sand dunes is a small beach bar which makes a good stopping place.

From here you can walk along to **Moll Morrig** and the beaches of **Illetas** and **Levant,** which have now been declared legal for nude bathing, but do be careful of the hot sun. Certainly if you wish to see untrodden sands and nothing else but sea and sky, this is the place. Formentera is still singularly unspoilt; perhaps this is the reason why so many of the inhabitants have been known to live to a great age. Because of the lack of fresh water, development is limited but one wonders if it will be long before this is overcome. In the meantime enjoy nature's sands and sea. At the extreme northern tip are the sands called **Trucadors** that lead to the island of **Espalmador.**

Cana Costa and La Sabina

Should you have time, spare a few moments to visit the island's oldest known construction, a dolmen (prehistoric stone circle) which lies at **Cana Costa,** between the La Sabina road and the salt lake. It's not very easy to locate as it is about 200m off the road behind a gate. A shelter has been erected to protect the limestone megalithic structure from the elements and a small wall around the site prevents inquisitive visitors from damaging this archaeological discovery. The excavations are not yet complete and little knowledge has been made public. One wonders if further digs will reveal any historic treasures.

On returning to **La Sabina,** take a look at this peaceful port with its recently planted palm trees and newly extended piers. Maybe you will see an old peasant lady, dressed in black and wearing a straw hat, sitting on the jetty with a fishing rod in her hands. She will hardly glance at the line of holidaymakers noisily embarking for Ibiza; for her, catching the evening meal is more important. This is Formentera.

Near La Sabina, undeveloped dunes with the occasional beach bar provide good swimming, walking and solitude.

Finale

Ibiza and Formentera are islands of contrast, where yesterday's history blends with modern progress. The easy going Ibicencos are a people who, despite a troubled history of marauding corsairs forever invading their shores to pillage and plunder, now show today's visitors a quiet welcome that is friendly and tolerant.

Holidaymakers have much to enjoy here, for the islands are bathed in brilliant sunshine for most of the year, offering miles of golden sands with warm seas that are sheltered by sweet pinewoods. Along the quiet roads, small villages with white fortified churches, offer interest and peaceful shopping. Beautiful and fertile valleys are filled with orange groves and sheep grazing. All are places to rest and relax. For the more energetic, sports of all kinds are available and the cheerful hotels and towns provide entertainments day and night for young and old to enjoy.

The fun islands of Ibiza and Formentera are for memorable holidays. We hope that your stay here will give you the happiness and contentment that you are seeking.

Appendix A
Spanish/English Vocabulary

Public signs and notices

abierto	open
aseo	toilet
caballeros	gentlemen
cerrado	closed
empuje	push
entrada	entrance
libre	free/vacant
muelle	quay
ocupado	engaged
privado	private
salida	depart/way out
senoras	ladies
se alquilar	to rent
se prohibe	forbidden
servicio	toilet
se vende	for sale
se prohibe estacioner	no parking
se prohibe fumar	no smoking
tire	pull

Drinks

beer	*cerveza*
coffee/black	*café solo*
Coffee/white	*café con leche*
gin	*ginebra*
ice	*hielo*
sherry	*jerez*
squash	*zumo*
tea	*té*
water	*agua*
wine dry	*vino seco*
red	*vino tinto*
sweet	*vino dulce*
white	*vino blanco*

Shops and places

bakery	*panaderia*
butcher's shop	*carnicería*
cake shop	*pastelería*
chemist	*farmacia*
church	*iglesia*
cinema	*cine*
dairy	*lecheria*
fishmonger	*pescadería*
grocer	*alimentacion*
ironmonger	*ferreteria*
library	*biblioteca*
market	*mercado*
post office	*correos*
shoe shop	*zapatería*
stationer	*papeleria*
theatre	*teatro*
town hall	*ayuntamiento*
view point	*mirador*

Restaurant

Bill	*cuenta*
bottle	*botella*
breakfast	*desayuno*
cup	*taza*
dinner	*cena*
drink	*bebida*
fork	*tenedor*
glass	*vaso*
knife	*cuchillo*
lunch	*almuerzo*
plate	*plato*
sandwich	*bocadillo*
spoon	*cuchara*
table	*mesa*
tip	*propina*
waiter	*camarero*

Useful words

all	*todo*
before	*antes*
behind	*detras*
big	*grande*
cold	*frio*
everybody	*todos*
fast	*rapido*
food	*alimento*
good	*bueno*
here	*aqui*
high	*alto*
hot	*caliente*
how many?	*cuantos*
how much?	*cuanto*
left (direction)	*izquierda*
like	*como*
little (quantity)	*poco*
lost	perdido
many	*mas*
near	*cerca*
no	*no*
old	*viejo*
please	*por favor*
right (direction)	*derecha*
slow	*lento*
Soon	*pronto*
thank you	*gracias*
too many	*demasiados*
too much	*demasiado*
under	*debajo*
up	*arriba*
very	*muy*
well	*bien*
when?	*cuando*
why?	*por que*
without	*sin*
with	*con*
yes	*si*

Days of the week

Sunday	*Domingo*
Monday	*Lunes*
Tuesday	*Martes*
Wednesday	*Miercoles*
Thursday	*Jueves*
Friday	*Viernes*
Saturday	*Sabado*

Months

January	*Enero*
February	*Febrero*
March	*Marzo*
April	*Abril*
May	*May*
June	*Junio*
July	*Julio*
August	*Agosto*
September	*Septiembre*
October	*Octubre*
November	*Noviembre*
December	*Diciembre*

Numbers

one	*uno, una*
two	*dos*
three	*tres*
four	*cuatro*
five	*cinco*
six	*seis*
seven	*siete*
eight	*ocho*
nine	*nueve*
ten	*diez*

Food

apple	*manzana*	mushrooms	*setas*
banana	*platano*	mussels	*mejillónes*
beef	*vaca*	mustard	*mostaza*
biscuit	*galleta*	oil	*aceite*
bread	*pan*	olives	*aceitunas*
butter	*mantequilla*	onions	*cebollas*
cabbage	*col*	orange	*naranja*
caramel pudding	*flan*	peach	melocoton
carrots	*zanahorias*	pear	*pera*
cauliflower	*coliflor*	peas	*guisantes*
cheese	*queso*	pepper	*pimienta*
chicken	*pollo*	pork	*cerda*
chop	*chuleta*	potatoes	*patatas*
cream	*nata*	rice	*arroz*
cucumber	*pepino*	salad	*ensalada*
egg	*huevo*	salt	*sal*
fish	*pescado*	sauce	*salsa*
french beans	*judias verde*	sausages	*chorizo*
grapes	*uvas*	shrimps	*gambas*
ham	*jamón*	strawberries	*fresas*
ice cream	*helados*	sugar	*azucar*
lamb	*cordero*	toast	*tostado*
lemon	*limon*	veal	*ternara*
lobster	*langosta*	vegetables	*verduras*
marmalade	*mermelada*	vinegar	*vinagre*

Appendix B
Wind Force: the Beaufort Scale*

B'fort No.	Wind Descrip.	Effect on land	Effect on sea	Wind Speed knots	mph	kph	Wave height (m)†
0	Calm	Smoke rises vertically	Sea like a mirror	less than 1			-
1	Light air	Direction shown by smoke but not by wind vane	Ripples with the appearance of scales; no foam crests	1-3	1-3	1-2	-
2	Light breeze	Wind felt on face; leaves rustle; wind vanes move	Small wavelets; crests do not break	4-6	4-7	6-11	0.15-0.30
3	Gentle breeze	Leaves and twigs in motion wind extends light flag	Large wavelets; crests begin to break; scattered white horses	7-10	8-12	13-19	0.60-1.00
4	Moderate breeze	Small branches move; dust and loose paper raised	Small waves, becoming longer; fairly frequent white horses	11-16	13-18	21-29	1.00-1.50
5	Fresh breeze	Small trees in leaf begin to sway	Moderate waves; many white horses; chance of some spray	17-21	19-24	30-38	1.80-2.50
6	Strong breeze	Large branches in motion; telegraph wires whistle	Large waves begin to form; white crests extensive; some spray	22-27	25-31	40-50	3.00-4.00

7	Near gale	Whole trees in motion; difficult to walk against wind	Sea heaps up; white foam from breaking waves begins to be blown in streaks	28-33 32-38	51-61 4.00-6.00
8	Gale	Twigs break off trees; progress impeded	Moderately high waves; foam blown in well-marked streaks	34-40 39-46	63-74 5.50-7.50
9	Strong gale	Chimney pots and slates blown off	High waves; dense streaks of foam; wave crests begin to roll over; heavy spray	41-47 47-54	75-86 7.00-9.75
10	Storm	Trees uprooted; considerable structural damage	Very high waves, overhanging crests; dense white foam streaks; sea takes on white appearance; visibility affected	48-56 55-63	88-100 9.00-12.50
11	Violent storm	Widespread damage, seldom experienced in England	Exceptionally high waves; dense patches of foam; wave crests blown into froth; visibility affected	57-65 64-75	101-110 11.30-16.00
12	Hurricane	Winds of this force encountered only in Tropics	Air filled with foam & spray; visibility seriously affected	65+ 75+	120+ 13.70+

---

* Introduced in 1805 by Sir Francis Beaufort (1774-1857) hydrographer to the Navy
† First figure indicates average height of waves; second figure indicates maximum height.

Appendix C
Useful Conversion Tables, Imperial/Metric

Distance/Height

feet	ft or m	metres
3.281	1	0.305
6.562	2	0.610
9.843	3	0.914
13.123	4	1.219
16.404	5	1.524
19.685	6	8.829
22.966	7	2.134
26.247	8	2.438
29.528	9	2.743
32.808	10	3.048
65.617	20	8.096
82.081	25	7.620
164.05	50	15.25
328.1	100	30.5
3281.	1000	305.

miles	**km or mls**	kilometres
0.621	1	1.609
1.243	2	3.219
1.864	3	4.828
2.486	4	6.437
3.107	5	8.047
3.728	6	9.656
4.350	7	11.265
4.971	8	12.875
5.592	9	14.484
6.214	10	16.093
12.428	20	32.186
15.534	25	40.234
31.069	50	80.467
62.13	100	160.93
621.3	1000	1609.3

Weight

pounds	**kg or lb**	kilograms
2.205	1	0.454
4.409	2	0.907
8.819	4	1.814
13.228	6	2.722
17.637	8	3.629
22.046	10	4.536
44.093	20	9.072
55.116	25	11.340
110.231	50	22.680
220.462	100	45.359

Your weight in kilos

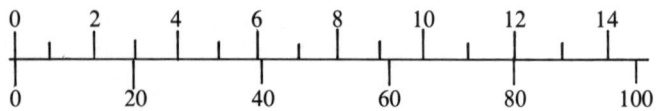

Liquids

gallons	**gal or l**	litres
0.220	1	4.546
0.440	2	9.092
0.880	4	18.184
1.320	6	27.276
1.760	8	36.368
2.200	10	45.460
4.400	20	90.919
5.500	25	113.649
10.999	50	227.298
21.998	100	454.596

Some handy equivalents for self caterers

1 oz	25 g	1 fluid ounce	25 ml
4 oz	125 g	¼ pt. (1 gill)	142 ml
8 oz	250 g	½ pt.	284 ml
1 lb	500 g	¾ pt.	426 ml
2.2 lb	1 kilo	1 pt.	568 ml
		1¾ pints	1 litre

Tyre pressure

lb per sq in	kg per sq cm
14	0.984
16	1.125
18	1.266
20	1.406
22	1.547
24	1.687
26	1.828
28	1.969
30	2.109
40	2.812

Temperature

centigrade	fahrenheit
0	32
5	41
10	50
20	68
30	86
40	104
50	122
60	140
70	158
80	176
90	194
100	212

Dress sizes

Size	bust/hip inches	bust/hip centimetres
8	30/32	76/81
10	32/34	81/86
12	34/36	86/91
14	36/38	91/97
16	38/40	97/102
18	40/42	102/107
20	42/44	107/112
22	44/46	112/117
24	46/48	117/122

Oven temperatures

Electric	Gas mark	Centigrade
225	¼	110
250	½	130
275	1	140
300	2	150
325	3	170
350	4	180
375	5	190
400	6	200
425	7	220
450	8	230

Appendix D: Bibliography

Arthur Foss *Ibiza and Menorca,* 1975. Faber. ISBN 057 110 4878

Frommer *Spain and Morocco,* 1981. Simon and Schuster. ISBN 0 671 41423 2

Dana Facaros and Michael Pauls *Mediterranean Island Hopping,* 1981. Sphere Books Ltd. ISBN 0 89526 847 7

Heinzel, Fitter and Parslow *The Birds of Britain and Europe,* 1979. Collins. ISBN 0 00 219210 1

Anthony Bonner *Plants of the Balearic Islands,* 1982. Editorial Moll, Palma, Majorca. ISBN 84 273 0423 4

Index

Place names on Formentera indicated by (Fo). Page references to photographs and maps appear in **bold** type.

accommodation 32 – 9; winter 15
air travel 23 – 4
Atalaya (mountain) 121, 122

Balafi 125
banks 58
bars 75
beaches 20 – 2; *see also under names of individual beaches*
bicycles 51 – 2, 80
birds 102 – 3
Birds of Britain and Europe (Heinzel, Fitter and Parslow) 103
Bonner, Anthony: *Plants of the Balearic Islands* 102
bowling 80
British Consul 56
budgeting 17
bull fighting 80
buses 52 – 3

Cabo Berberia (Fo) 147
cafes 75
Cala Bassa 20, 123
Cala Carbo 122
Cala Conta 20, 123
Cala D'Hort 20, 122
Cala Llonga 20, 136
Cala Moli 122
Cala Nova 20, 140
Cala Pada 20, 138
Cala Portinatx 20, 127 – 8
Cala Sahona (Fo) 22, 146
Cala Salida 20
Cala San Vicente 22, **42**, 141 – 2
Cala Talamanca 20, 135
Cala Tarida 22, 122
Cala Vedella 22, 122
Cala Xarraca 127
Camel Cellar 119
camping 40 – 1

Cana Costa (Fo) 152
cars: hire of 50 – 1; servicing and repairs 48
Casa de la Curia (Ibiza town) 84
Castell D'es Puig 124
children, facilities for 41, 43 – 4
church services 56
cigarettes 17
cinemas 86
climate 13; chart 14; wind force chart 158 – 9
clothes and personal effects 16; shopping for 66
coaches: excursions 54 – 5; to ferries 30
complaints 63
conversion charts 160 – 4
cost of living 17
Cova Santa 18, 119
Cueva Es Cuyeram 142
Cuevas de Can Marca 131
Cuevas de las Fontanellas 132
Cuevas Xeroni (Fo) 19, 149
currency 18, 58

Dalt Vila 18, 104 – 9
dancing (Ibizan) 97
dentists 61
discotheques 85
diving 81
doctors 60 – 1
dogs 103
dolmens 152
donkey treks 131
drinks and drinking 74 – 5, 86
drinking water 59
driving 47 – 8
duty free goods 24

electricity 59
entertainment 84 – 6

Es Calo (Fo) 150
Es Cana 22, **139**, 140
Es Cavallet 22, 119
Es Cubells 18, 121–2
Es Figueral 22, 141
Es Pujols **21**, 22, 147, **148**, 149
Estang des Peix (lagoon, Fo) 145
Estang Pudent (lagoon, Fo) 145
estate agents 45
excursions: by coach 54–5

ferries: coach services to 30; from Europe 25, 26–7; Ibiza 54; inter–island 23, 29; rail services to 30; roads to ferry ports 25–6
fiestas 98–9
Figueretes 117
Finca Can Truy: folk dancing 96
fire precautions 59
fishing 81
flowers and plants 99–102
folk music and dance 96–9
food 17, 70–3 *see also* restaurants
football 81
Formentera: buses 53; fiestas 98, 99; map **144**; taxis 52

galleries 84
geographical location and features 12–13
glass–blowing factory 124
go–karting 81
golf 81

hairdressers 59
health 59–60 *see also* medical services
historical background 87–91
holiday villages 32
horse racing 81–2
hotels 32–8; facilities for children 43
hunting 82

Ibiza: fiestas 98, 99; maps **46**; east **134**; north **126**; south west **116**
Ibiza (town) 104–15; buses 53; car hire 51; casino 85; cathedral 107; Dalt Vila 104–9; fiestas 98; La Marina 111; markets 65; modern town 111–13; museums 84, 105, 107 113; police 63; post office 57; Puig des Molins 19, 87–8, 113; Sa Pena 109, **110**; taxis 52; tourist office 18; yacht clubs 31
Ibizan way of life 94–5
Illetas (Fo) 22, 152
Isla Conjera 12, 123
Isla de Ahorcados 13, 145
Isla de Tagomago 12, 141
Isla Espalmador 13, 145
Isla Espardel 13
Isla Vedra 13, 122, 145

Jesus 135–6

La Canal 118
La Mola (Fo) 150
La Sabina (Fo) 19, 145, 152; car hire 51
Las Salinas 18, 118–19
Las Salinas (Fo) 150, 152
laundry 60
Levante (Fo) 22, 152
liqueurs: distillery 133
Lladro porcelain 66

Macabich Y Llobet, Isidoro (statue) 106
magazines 62
maps 47; Formentera **144**; Ibiza **46**; east **134**; north **126**; south west **116**
markets 65–6
medical services 60–1
Mirador Es Calo (Fo) 19
Moll Morrig (Fo) 152
Monte Cristo 124
mopeds 51–2

Morna Valley 140
motorcaravanning 41
museums and galleries
  Casa de la Curia 84;
  Museo Arqueologico (Dalt
  Vila) 84, 107; Museo
  Arqueologico (Puig des
  Molins) 84, 113; Museo
  Arte Contemporaneo 84, 105;
  Museo Catedral 84, 107
music 96 – 7; bars 85 – 6

Na Xamena 131
national holidays 99
newspapers 62
nightlife 85 – 6
nudist beaches 20, 22
Nuestra Senora del Pilar (Fo)
  150

opticians 61 – 2

package holidays 24, 39
passports 17
pearls, man – made 68, 142
petrol stations: Ibiza 50,
  127, 142; Formentera 145
photography 16
Playa Arenal (Fo) 20, 149
Playa Cavallet 22, 119
Playa de Mitjorn (Fo) 22, 149
Playa del Figueral 22, 141
Playa D'En Bossa 22, 117 – 8
Playa Es Cana 22, **139**, 140
Playa Es Pujols (Fo) **21**, 22,
  147, **148**, 149
Playa Las Salinas 22, 119
Playa San Miguel 22
police 62 – 3
population 92
Port D'Es Torrent 22, 123
Portinatx 20, 127 – 8
postal services 56 – 7
property purchase 45
Puerto de San Miguel 128, 131
Puerto La Sabina (Fo) 19, 145
  152; car hire 51
Puig D'en Valls 133

Puig des Molins 19, 87 – 8, 113
  museum 84
Puig Guillem (Fo) 146
Punta Arabi 19; Hippy Market
  140
Punta Pinet 123

radio 63 – 5
rail services: to ferries 30
restaurants 75 – 9
riding 82
road signs 49
roads: to ferry ports 25 – 6;
  on the islands 47
Roca Llisa 136

S'Aigua Blanca 141
S'Argamassa 138
sailing 82 *see also* yacht
  clubs
San Antonio 19; 123 – 4; buses
  53; car hire 51; fiestas
  98, 99; information office
  18; market 66; police 63;
  taxis 52; yacht club 31
San Augustin 123
San Carlos 140
San Fernando (Fo) 147
San Francisco 118
San Francisco Javier (Fo) 19,
  145 – 6; police 63; post
  office 57; tourist office
  18
San Jorge 118
San Jose 19, 121; fiestas 98
San Juan Bautista 19, 127,
  142; fiesta 99
San Lorenzo 125
San Mateo 132
San Miguel 19, 128, **129**; buses
  53; fiesta 98; folk dancing
  97; market 66
San Rafael 19, 124
Santa Eulalia del Rio 19,
  136 – 8; buses 53; car hire
  51; fiestas 98, 99; police
  63; taxis 52; tourist
  office 18

Santa Eulalia del Rio (river) 12
Santa Gertrudis 131
Santa Innes 19, 132
scooters 51–2
sea excursions 82
Ses Roques Altes 122
Ses Salinas (Fo) 20; beach 22
shopping 65–8
souvenirs 66–8
Spanish Consulate (London) 17
Spanish/English vocabulary 155–7
Spanish Tourist Office (London) 17
sports 80–4
squash 82
standard of living 92
swimming 83 *see also* beaches

taxis 52
telegraph 58
telephones 57–8
television 69
telex 58
temperature chart 14
tennis 83
time 69
tipping 55, 69
tobacco 17
tourist information 17–18
tourist season 14–15
tourists 11, 92
travel agents: British 24; local 44
trees 99, 101
Talamanca 135
Trucadors (Fo) 152

veterinary services 45
videos 69

walking 83
water, drinking 59
waterskiing 84
wildlife 102–3
wind force chart 158–9
windsurfing 84

yacht clubs 31